Seasons of Prayer

Scott Taylor

Parson's Porch Books
www.parsonsporchbooks.com

Seasons of Prayer
ISBN: Softcover 978-1-951472-41-2
Copyright © 2020 by Scott Taylor

All rights reserved. No part of this book may be reproduced or transmitted in any form or by any means, electronic or mechanical, including photocopying, recording, or by any information storage and retrieval system, without permission in writing from the publisher.

Seasons of Prayer

Contents

Acknowledgements.. 8
Introduction... 11

Winter Season - A Time of Anticipation and Hope

Tommy visits Bennie and the Deuce.. 15
    Awaiting the Bringer of Hope 19
    In Preparation... 21
    Preparing the Way.. 23
    Our Loving God.. 24
    You'll Wake the Baby... 26
    The Gift... 28
    On the Run Again... 30
    They Went to See... 32
    Jacob's Stone Pillow... 34
    An Epiphany of Light... 36
    A Voice was Heard in Ramah... 38
    I Am Forgiven.. 40
    Abundant Hospitality... 42
    You Know What's Funny, God?..................................... 44
    And the Wine Flows... 46
    Guide Us, Lord 48
    We Pray Your Realm Comes Soon................................. 50
    Transfigured... 51

Spring Season – A Time of Penitence and Joy

Tommy's Pain and Joy.. 55
    Obedience is as Obedience Does................................... 58
    Turning About.. 60
    Anything Can Happen at a Well..................................... 62
    We Confess... 64
    Deliverance from Blindness... 66
    How Many Times Must I Tell You?................................ 68
    Peace Be With You... 70
    Your Light Will Show 72
    I Wouldn't Recognize You... 74
    In the Worrying.. 76
    Suddenly 78

Stewardship is a Gift 80
Your Spirit at Work 82
A Surprising God 84
for Our Sins are Great 86
Re-collected 88
Mother to Us All 90
Change Is Hard, Lord 92
Just One Spirit 94
In Memoriam 95

Summer Season - A Time for Service and Love

Tommy and Change 99
Forgive Our Foolishness 101
We Praise You, God 103
The Sound of the Wind 105
For the Times He Was Bold 107
You Do Not Fit Well into Boxes 109
Salt and Light 111
A Call of Creation 113
But You're Not 114
What if Everyone Repents? 116
Set Us Free 118
O Lord, Hear Our Prayers 119
Another Day 121
As You Promised 123
Pray for Us Sinners 125
Blind Like Jesus 127
Go and Do Likewise 129
Thin Space 131
Who Is Our Neighbor? 133
Help Us to See 135
Think About Today 137
The Water is a Scary Place 139
Kernels of Hope 141
And the World was Fed 143
God, Demons are Scary 144
Bread of Life 146
And We Reply 148
Lord, She's Here Again 150
We Are One in Christ 151

Fall Season - A Time for Gratitude and Peace

Tommy gets Honest 155
    Like a Wayward Child 159
    Lord, This is Hard for Us 161
    Still You Send Us 163
    But We Doubt 165
    Be With Us, Lord 167
    How Many Times? 169
    Be Still 170
    Welcome the Visitors 172
    Love One Another 174
    Choices 176
    I Wanted To 178
    Take Our Stoney Hearts 180
    A Both-And Kind of Guy 181
    Help Us to Keep Focused 183
    Abundance 185
    Like the Rich Young Man 187
    You Are There 189
    Under the Oaks at Mamre 190
    The Voice 192
    Love Comes First 194
    Thanksgiving Every Day 196
    They Were Lovers of Peace 198
    Letting Go 200
    Bless Our Hearts, Lord 202
    We Thank You, Lord 204

Scripture Index 206

Acknowledgements

The impetus for this collection came principally from Cathy Feldotto and Kay Northcutt whose persistent requests for it have remained stuck in my consciousness long after the end of my ministry at First Christian Church in Grand Island, NE. Without it, I'm afraid the normal entropy of retirement may have meant the pile of prayers sat on the shelf forever! I guess we'll never know. Thanks, Cathy and Kay!

Certainly they weren't alone in their request. The wonderful folks at Grand Island are the community within which most of these prayers and stories were birthed. The Tommy stories especially owe their generation to the congregation. Those stories also provided the seasonal flavor that led to the title, *Seasons of Prayer*.

Of course, one's spiritual formation spans a lifetime and is foundational to whatever form the prayers may take so I want to recognize the strong contribution from all of the wonderful mentors I've enjoyed over the years. The pastors who have nurtured me well: Ray Nixon, John Henry Cain, Barney McLaughlin, Gary Mitchell, Leslie Dotson, Roy Fleshman, Ann Jordan, Rob Crawford, Jerry Deffenbaugh, Leslie Penrose, Melinda Foster, Chuck Shorow, John Imbler, Rick Lowery, and Sharon Watkins. You all prepared me well for parish ministry and these prayers stem from that planting.

And, as any good farmer knows, producing a crop takes much more than simply planting so I need to thank the many folks in Nebraska who supported me: Tim and Ginny Adams, Jim Gordon, Ken Moore, Dustin Bower, Lew Champ, Michael Stein, and Judy Allen Dalton. Special thanks to everyone at First Christian Church, Grand Island, as their support was a blessing. I doubt they fully understood but one that I'm extremely grateful for having received.

Even before Nebraska, I was nurtured and cared for by friends and faculty at Phillips Theological Seminary, Tulsa, OK. My thanks go to Joe Bessler, my teacher and mentor, to all the other professors who guided us all, notably Rick Lowery, Dennis Smith, Brandon Scott, Ellen Blue, John Thomas and Nancy Pittman. A special thanks goes to Kay Northcutt who asked us 'let me see your eyes' to be certain we were taking in everything she had to give as we crafted beginning prayers as part of her preaching class. A special thanks also to Sheri Curry and Sue Williams who were my partners as we led morning prayers during our time in seminary. Their example and dedication have guided me ever since. Thank you especially to Bill Kahler and Michael Bowers who graciously read drafts and offered helpful insights.

Finally, a deep debt of gratitude is owed to Chuck Peek who took the time to read and critique this work at several stages; his encouragement and labor have taken this from a pile of pages on a shelf to an actual coherent collection. Thank you, Chuck, I will attempt to always assuage your appetite for homemade sauerkraut!

Introduction

Over the past decade, I've written pastoral prayers for worship each week. These were written in the heat of the moment, so to speak. Usually composed early Sunday morning after the week-long digestion of scripture, they are graced with current news and whatever other sources fly by on Facebook, television, etc. Moreover, they are imbued with the weather of the day: rainy, snowy, hot, sunny, cloudy days that greet us and build our patience. As I prepared for worship, these are the words that came to me, the words that seemed appropriate to bless the congregation, the words that connected ancient scripture with our modern lives.

So, necessarily, there are references to local and national organizations that we worked with and supported. CWS is Church World Service which also includes their CROP Walk. CWS is an international group dedicated to ending hunger around the world. Relay for Life is a charity event in support of the American Cancer Society. Hope Harbor supports folks recovering from addiction. Kamp Kaleo is the church camp for UCC/DOC regions. In Oklahoma, Agape` Mission, Concern, and Elder Care support folks in need across all ages. The work we did for these events and groups was a vital part of our ministry and that is reflected in some of the prayers in this collection.

Each prayer is identified by title and followed by the date written along with the scripture for that date. Several prayers have indications for moments of silence. In our use, this was usually a silent pause of 1-2 minutes, sufficient for several breath prayers or to simply relax in solitude.

Were the prayers successful? Who knows? Did God speak to us all during our time together every Sunday morning? Certainly. At least it seems so to me. Will they speak to you? Who knows?! Will God speak to you as you sit with these prayers? I suspect so although I offer no guarantee other than that you will spend time in God's presence. Of course, if you believe in an ever-present God, this is a pretty solid guarantee even if you never get past this page of the collection!

Oh, by the way, if you run into Tommy somewhere down the road, say hello to him for me. Thanks for your support and love!

Rev. Dr. Scott R. Taylor
Bartlesville, OK
www.srtaylor.us

Winter Season

A Time for Anticipation and Hope

Tommy visits Bennie and the Deuce

Well, let me tell you a story. It's about my friend, Tommy. Some of you know Tommy, I've talked about him over the years, but some of you haven't met him before so I'll give you a little background.

Tommy is an old friend of mine; I met him many years ago when I was doing some consulting work for a company over in Spencerville. Ever been to Spencerville? Sure you have - it's that small town on the way from here to there. It's a pretty little town with a nice town square and old streets lined with even older oak and maple trees. It was beautiful in the fall, but the leaves are all down by now. There's still the smell of burning leaves on the breeze; reminds me of when I was a child and we burned the fall leaves in our backyard.

I first met Tommy when he helped me with a flat tire, taking the tire over to Red's Auto Service without me even asking. He's thoughtful like that, at least he seems that way to me. Plenty other folks found him a little strange, maybe even slow, but I like him well enough. I usually run into Tommy at the Buttermilk Café where Elvira watches over the comings and goings of the delightful assortment of characters any small town holds. You can see the whole square as you look out the front window where Elvira always displays a slice of pie along with a faded menu on a checkerboard clothed table.

Recently, we ran into Tommy while we were getting gas in Concordia. He said he was returning home after visiting his grandfather who lives in a nursing home outside Wichita. We had some time, so we went to McDonald's, got some coffee - well, I had one of the fancy Mochas they make - and had a nice little visit. I asked how everything was down at the Buttermilk Café, how were Elvira and all her regulars; he said they were all fine although Elvira needed a little more help cleaning tables, so he'd do that when she wasn't watching.

He mentioned how Javier Garcia had gotten all the wreaths and lights up for the annual Christmas Pageant next weekend. Javier had been in town for a while, but it was good to see he'd gotten on with the County Agency as I knew their family needed all the help they could get.

Then I asked him, "Did you go down to Walmart last week for the Black Friday sales to get some good bargains?"

Now, at this, Tommy did one of the things that made some people think he was kind of slow. He just stared for a moment like this was a totally new thought to him, like he was from some other country or planet and had never heard of Walmart or Black Friday or even bargains! You couldn't really tell if he was looking at you or just slightly over your shoulder, and it would seem like it would go on for several minutes; everything was suspended in time. I'm sure it only lasted for seconds but it was disconcerting if you didn't know him.

Then he'd just smile and blink his eyes before speaking quietly.

"No, what would they have had down there to be thankful for that I haven't got right here? Oh, I went and got a turkey for Harvey to fix for the bridge people last week but 'Black Friday'? Seems like a kinda mean thing to call the day after Thanksgiving," he opined.

And then he smiled at me again. You know, I'd tell you what Tommy was wearing if I could ever remember it! His smile is what he wore best and what I remember most.

"Besides, the really important thing is just a few weeks or so away. Baby Jesus is coming." Tommy said with evident relish.

I nodded, thinking how I'd barely made it through Thanksgiving let alone gotten anywhere near ready for Christmas and here Tommy was already filled with anticipation and hope. We sipped some coffee, not saying anything, then I asked, "So, what were you thankful for this Thanksgiving, Tommy?"

"I'm thankful for Bennie and the Deuce!" he said positively.

He started out by telling me how Elvira at the Buttermilk Café closes for Thanksgiving - she visits her daughter's family on the other side of the state, I think primarily to see her two grandchildren, a boy and little sister. So Spencerville is pretty quiet. It's really quiet this year because Bennie and the Deuce are in the county lockup in Sheriff Hickersen's office. The Deuce is a smalltime hood, a conman and a no-goodnik; Bennie is his sidekick. Bennie's not a bad dude, just kind of simple. He's tall, heavyset and really strong. No one's sure why he hangs around with the Deuce but there's some kind of connection. The Deuce, who's always looking for an angle, uses Bennie all the time but still has some sort of loyalty to him.

But, like Tommy said, they're both in the slammer now. The Deuce got caught selling iPods that he and Bennie had 'picked up' somewhere, namely, off the Radio Shack in the little strip mall just west of town. They hadn't actually broken in, just happened to be around as the delivery truck was unloading! Due to the holidays, they couldn't be arraigned until next week so Sheriff Hickersen had to hold onto them. Thanksgiving in prison seemed like it would be a lonely affair.

Tommy sort of smirked and said he chose to go visit Bennie and the Deuce. He didn't have anything to bring them except a can of cranberry sauce and a couple spoons. It was strange Tommy would even go because everyone assumed that that time Tommy's apartment was robbed, Bennie and the Deuce had something to do with it. But Tommy didn't judge them, or, maybe he forgave them; I don't know.

Of course, the Deuce wanted to know what was Tommy's angle - what was he going to get out of this visit? And if he wasn't getting anything then, as far as the Deuce was concerned, he was just a chump.

But Bennie, normally pretty taciturn and quiet, told the Deuce to leave it alone; he was thankful for the cranberry sauce and for the visit. He told the Deuce, "Tommy never did nothing to us and he didn't have to do this. Thanks, Tommy." Tommy was just glad to share with someone who needed a little love and compassion - that made it 'Thanksgiving' as far as he was concerned.

Another one of his over the shoulder gazes and then he spoke again. "And I'm thankful for you. And for Javier and Benny and Elvira and for my granddad and ... peanut butter!"

I laughed along with him saying, "Peanut Butter?! You like peanut butter?"

"No so much - but the squirrels sure do! It was their 'turkey and gravy' on Thanksgiving and they'll think it's a fine Christmas gift too. Them and the birds look so pretty against the trees and fallen leaves still on the ground, I can't imagine anything much more beautiful... well, except for the candles on Christmas Eve shining on the manger." Tommy smiled and lifted his eyebrows conspiratorially at me and said, "If you look just right, you can see God all over the place."

After the quiet wore off, Tommy hopped up and said, "Gee, it was great to see you but I've gotta run, Red's got an old tire fixed for Elvira and I promised to get back in time to put it on her car so she could drive to church tomorrow!"

With better clarity from the caffeine and greater hope from Tommy, we headed across the bridge and through the woods to go home, thankful all the way.

Awaiting the Bringer of Hope

Lord, I hope you come soon.
We wait in the darkness,
chilly and weary
of our struggles.

We'd like to say
that we'll get to you
once the shopping is done,
the house is cleaned,
all the cookies are baked,
and the presents wrapped.

But then the bills will come
and the wrapping paper will
need to be gleaned
for next year
and there's
next year's Christmas cards
to buy on sale.

And of course school starts
again
driving teachers and students
into the cold night
with homework and
glee club and yearbook
and then there's March madness...

But this is exactly what you
break into, Lord of light,
Bringer of Hope,
Peace,
Joy and Love!

It is not that
we need to make room
for you, rather,
that we need to recognize
and cherish the gift
you bring into our busy midst!

Thank you, God, thank you.

Amen.

First Sunday of Advent - 12/2/12

In Preparation

Snow: crisp, white snow covers
the ground this morning.
Slippery, icy, wintery -
almost like a Christmas card
bought for a dear friend
if only we can get past
our worries about driving safely!

Maybe staying home
warm in our fuzzy blankets
would be the thing to do.

But we are here, God.
Thankful for those who arrived
early to shovel and plow.

Or maybe we're here
because we need you to come
into our hearts and minds,
chilled as they are with
worries and fears.

We long for peace
while simultaneously
crying foul! Crying
if only 'they' would
do something, act better,
acknowledge our rightness
we could find peace.

But that's not your peace, Lord.

We pray this morning
that we reduce the mountains
of worry that keep us
from praising you.

We pray this morning
that we smooth
the rough places in our souls
that drag us down.

We pray this morning
that we make the way straight
to our hearts, a smooth
path for you, dear Jesus.

And we know that your peace
will fill us then,
as the shepherd holds the lamb
close to his heart.

Thank you, God, thank you.

Amen.

12/4/11
Isa 40:1-11; Psalm 85:1-2, 8-13

Preparing the Way

What did the prophet Isaiah say,
'Prepare the way of the Lord'?
God, it was many years
from Isaiah to John the Baptist
yet we hear their stories
as connected.

Tied to the same story
that you create eternally,
our stories also must
'Prepare the way of the Lord'

Still, we often feel
more like we're simply
wandering in the desert
and the details of our
daily life swamp the bigger story you tell.

Yet now, once more,
as the darkness closes us in,
we hear about birth
and bright stars
and shepherds
and a miraculous gift
given whether our home
is neat as a pin or messy as a stable.

Let us make the pathways straight,
fill the valleys and flatten the mountains,
smooth and straighten
our crooked ways
for the salvation of God is come!

Thank you, God, thank you.

Amen.

12/9/12
Luke 3:1-6

Our Loving God

This is a day of miracles
and love!
The Lord has come to his people
and redeemed them,
so we may serve without fear
in holiness and righteousness.

Yes, it is a day of love.

God, you know the way
you like to grab me with a phrase
as I'm reading scripture?
I love that.

And you know that thing you do
when someone needs help,
someone I don't know
and probably wouldn't choose
to know but they need
my help
anyway?
That way you have of
setting them right in front of me?
I love that, too.

And you know the way
sometimes someone tells me
I helped them
and I didn't
even know it?

You did that too
didn't you?
I love that.

Boy oh boy,
I don't know what I'd do
without you, God.

Thank you, God, thank you.

Amen.

12/18/11
Luke 1:67-79

You'll Wake the Baby

It's Christmas - Shhhh - you'll wake the baby.

The birth was - wondrous and yet . . .
It was like the whole world held its breath for a moment -
then there he was.

Is he going to love us? Yes - with a love like
there's no tomorrow and like all the tomorrows
there will ever be - all at the same time!

Mary, did you know?

On wrinkled sunlight and crisp hay
warm from a rest after the birth, you're here!
We'll name you Emmanuel, Emmanuel.

In our midst, you're here. We're not a big community,
but we'll love you and keep you safe.
We're off the beaten path so sometimes
it seems hard to get very many people to visit,
but we'll love you and keep you safe.

And sometimes, we're more family
than community.

We welcome each other more
than the stranger - you'll remind us about that, okay?
We'll serve food to hungry people,
we'll serve on community boards,
and all the places where our family world collides
with our community - because we love you.

All the gold, frankincense and myrrh we've got
will go to good use!

Ah, did you have to burp, little one?
Sometimes, life is hard and filled
with surprises and disappointments.
Some of us here today are holding
pain and sorrow inside;
I'll whisper your name for them.

Emmanuel, Emmanuel.

God is with us.

Amen.

Christmas Eve - 12/24/16

The Gift

God, I saw a star last night.
It was the biggest, brightest
star
I've ever seen!

And it looked for all the world
like a guidepost,
a marker, a sign of some sort,
announcing the unexpected.

I still see it's light in my heart.

We have waited in hope.
we have yearned for peace,
and danced with joy,
awash in the love
you give to us
with such abundance and abandon!

But Creator, if it is truly you
come into the world,
we've got to say
we expected something more -
something grander than
a simple star seen mostly
by shepherds and sheep.

A homeless baby doesn't
look like much lying still
in a manger.
And yet the starlight
from that brilliant star
still lingers in Mary's eyes
as she ponders all that happened.

Lord, it's peaceful now
and I just know that Joseph
appreciated that!
What a gift!
The light of the world
has come into the world
and even the brightest star
cannot overshadow Him!

Thank you, God, thank you.

Amen.

Christmas Day - 12/25/11
Luke 2:1-20

On the Run Again

God, just when we think
things are getting better,
the rug gets pulled out
again.
And again, we're on the run.

Sometimes, it feels like
we'll never get caught up,
that the hope we longed for
will never be realized.

Our childhood has been forsaken
and we weep,
for our youth is no more.

And yet, there you are, Lord.
Still fresh and new
each time we cry out
and turn to you, Jesus.

We turn to you
in our prayers for healing,
for all who are ill
or recovering from
sickness or surgery.

We turn to you
in our prayers for guidance and direction.
Lead us anew as we
plan how to live out
Your vision for us
at our Annual Planning Event.

We turn to you
in our prayers for peace.
Let it begin with us.
Let us practice
love for one another,
just as you commanded us,
so the whole world
will know Your Peace.

Thank you, God, thank you!

Amen.

12/29/13
Matt 2:13-23

They Went to See

You know, God
that this whole story about
angels and a pregnant, unwed
mother is a little
far-fetched.

Yet an angel visited shepherds
and terrorized them, something unusual
for men used to being
alone in the dark.

So they went to see.
So they went with joy
to see the babe, the Messiah
and they told everyone
what the angel told them.

What a story!
All were amazed, but
Mary kept her thoughts close,
pondering it all
just as we still ponder today.

We pray this day for the world,
a place big enough for all
yet small enough to cause us grief.
We pray for those suffering war;
bring us all peace.

We pray this day for our neighbors,
those we know and also those
we see but barely notice.
The homeless and poor,
the hard-working immigrant,
the babies they cuddle; we
pray for their future and hope.

We pray this day for our friends
in this church. We pray healing
for those sick and tired,
struggling with cancer and flu.
We include those in our
wider family suffering pain
and loss of loved ones.
Hold them safe in their sorrow.

Thank you, God, Thank you.

Amen.

12/28/14
Luke 2:8-20

Jacob's Stone Pillow

'Now I lay me down to sleep,
I pray the Lord my soul to keep'
God, how many times did I pray that?
How many times have I laid
down to sleep not praying at all?
Sometimes the weight of my
troubles feel like Jacob's stone pillow
and there's no hope
for anything
beyond a lonely, long night.

But even the Angels
have a stairway to you, O God.
They come and go,
assured that you go with them.

Go with us, God, let us know
that you are with us
always and forever.

We thank you, Lord
and pray for our mission team
going to Nicaragua
that their ministry
will be a blessing to all involved.

We thank you, Creator
and pray for our community,
for all who seek shelter during
the cold, winter months.
May we remember this in our
warm homes.

We thank you, Light of the world
and pray for our church.
Help us to think and think again
knowing you are with us
in this place just as you were
with Abraham and Isaac and Jacob and so many others!

Thank you, God, Thank you.

Amen.

New Year's Day - 1/3/16
Gen 28:10-17

An Epiphany of Light

Lord, Lord, it's dark
out here on the road
of life!

No shining stars
seem to appear when needed
and we blunder along
searching for a flashlight
only to find the batteries
are almost dead.

Then we are reminded
of the story of
three wise men
who followed the Star
and found an epiphany
of light in a little baby.

Jesus, light of the world,
we pray the light
of your love fill our weary hearts
shedding the load of guilt and fear
we try to carry in the darkness.

God, we pray the light
shine upon our
new church starts
here in the Nebraska Region.
May they be a beacon
to those in need.

Master builder,
we pray the light shine upon
this church, leading us
ever to do your will,
meeting the needs we can meet
even when we think

they're unreachable.

Abba,
we pray the light shine
into someone's heart today;
someone is struggling and afraid.
Let the light burst through
and warm them with hope.

Thank you, God, thank you.

Amen.

Epiphany - 1/6/13
Isaiah 60:1-6; Matt 2:1-12

A Voice was Heard in Ramah

God, we are a violent people
who don't listen very well!

How is "Thou shalt not kill."
hard to understand? And yet,
we overlook it with regularity-
painful regularity.

Oh God, we pray for the students and faculty
at Millard High School in Omaha.
We pray for Robert Butler, Jr., who killed himself after shooting Principal Curtis Case and Vice Principal Vicki Kaspar. We pray for their families, grieving the deaths
of their loved ones.

If that weren't enough for one week,
senseless violence tore through
Tucson yesterday and left six people dead and 13 critically injured including Rep. Gabrielle Giffords.

We pray for the dead; we pray for their families. We pray for the wounded - may your healing touch be with them.

Once more,
> "A voice was heard in Ramah,
> wailing and loud lamentation.
> Rachel weeping for her children;
> she refused to be consoled, because
> they are no more."

And yet, You, O God, are our strength.
Beyond the veil of violence,
a peaceful valley awaits and
we make straight the roadways and paths
in our praise to you.

You are ever with us,
in shopping malls and supermarkets,
high schools and beautiful parks;
You are our rock and our redeemer.

Thank you, God, thank you.

Amen.

1/9/11
Matt 3:13-17

I Am Forgiven

The water is chilly
and it shocks my breathe away-
I have nothing
to hold onto
except your grace, O God!

Will you be there
again?
and again?

Blessed Spirit
fill me with your loving
touch and sweet perfume!

My heart knows joy
and it is as if
the very heavens broke open
and you wrapped me gently
in your soft arms.

I am forgiven.

Forgiven to be able
to feed my friends,
to be able to feed the stranger.

Forgiven to be able
to love my neighbor
and let them be just
who they are.

Forgiven to be able
to face this morning
and tomorrow morning
and the next one after that.

The water is chilly but
your love and quiet voice
warm me and comfort me.

Now, I am your child.

Thank you, God, thank you.

Amen.

1/11/09
Mark 1:4-11

Abundant Hospitality

God, you like a good cook, don't you?
When you met Abraham under the oaks of Mamre,
you savored his abundant hospitality,
full and joyful,
Abraham's eyes dusty with sleep
so he saw only strangers-
but welcomed them anyway.

Mystery, we are the salt of your earth,
you have seasoned our world with life abundant
and we say, "Thank you."

Creator, we are the light of your world,
you overcame chaos
with the powerful words,
"Let there be light!"
and we say, "Thank you."

YHWH God, we are the work of your creation,
given to work and take care of it,
to be your stewards
and we say, "Thank you."

But are we truly thankful
if we hold onto our old ways
and let 800 million people starve
while over a billion are overweight?

What kind of a thanksgiving
lets us build walls that tear
families apart, that speaks
of 'us' and 'them' rather than 'we'?

What kind of a Thanksgiving Table
do we set when we aim
for Imperial peace, the peace
bought by violence?

God, you like a good cook
but sometimes, we won't follow
your recipe because we think
we don't have what it takes.

So thank you, God,
for your strength and mercy
when we find ways to
turn enemies into friends.

Thank you, Creator,
for your patience and grace
as we struggle with the differences
between "immigrant', 'illegal', and 'alien'.

Thank you, Mystery,
for your love that
loves us even when we
find it hard to love ourselves,
let alone that 'other' living
down the road or across town
or right next door.

Light and salt you ask for,
Master Chef; and we answer

Thank you, God, thank you.

Amen.

Minister's Week - 1/13/09
Gen 18:1-8

You Know What's Funny, God?

By the still smooth waters,
my soul rests.
There is love here. There is
peace here.

But God, my desires and plans sometimes
center solely on myself.
I'm sorry about that, but
you knew that all along, didn't you?

And you know what's funny, God?
I know my greatest joy
and peace when I
find myself caring for others,
really listening to your prayer,
'Thy will be done'.

You know what's funny, God?
When it's beautiful outside;
the glory of creation
makes my heart swell almost
to bursting and I ache with
joy that I'm a part of it all,
too.

You know what's funny, God?
There's still times when I turn away,
when my pride and foolish self
lust - there's no other word for it,
lust - for who knows what?

It might be for a donut, or a
new guitar, or another computer gizmo.
Whatever it is, it's just for me.

Your love for us is so hard
to believe, sometimes.

But then, when we'll relax and do something
for someone else, your love
gives them a hug better than we ever could!

So give us love, O God, so we
can love our children - our children
in our own families, and our children
in our community.

Give us love, O God, so we can
bring strength to those among us
suffering health problems. We need to always
let them know they are held
warm and
loved.

For you have called us, saying
'You are my child, my beloved'.

By your still smooth waters,
There is love.

Amen.

1/13/08
Matthew 3:13-17

And the Wine Flows

Lord, it's not your time.
It's not the miracle
that matters, it's the faith
it elicits and the way
we come to believe
you are
the Son of God!

Wine and more wine
flows as the miracle
points to a grand
wedding banquet!
You are the bridegroom
and we are your bride,
God's people.

And yet we confess that
it's often easier
to enjoy the wine
as a good trick well played.
Maybe we're too afraid
of what it might mean
to really believe.

We pray for belief
to fill our unbelief!
We pray for hope and relief
for the poor and hungry
in our community.
Because we believe, we'll
support Salvation Army.

Because we believe, we'll
build up Children's Church
and Play Day for the children
are yours, too!

Because we believe, we'll
pray for new churches
and for renewing churches, God,
Creator, Wisdom, Eternal Love!
You are doing new things
and we know it will be exciting!

Thank you, God, thank you.

Amen!

1/20/13
John 2:1-11

Guide Us, Lord

God, have mercy on us sinners.
We confess that we too often
take for granted our knowledge of you
assuming others
know you as we do.

We smile and go about our business
happily unaware that we might be
leading someone
far
from your path.

Guide us, Lord, gently or no,
to watch out
for the weak and confused.

You have set us free.
Christ, you have set us free
not for our own desires
but for service as you served.

We pray today for the children
of our congregation,
of our schools,
and of our community.
May we be models of your justice and peace.

We pray today for the elderly
in our community,
bound to nursing homes
and retirement communities
or just at home.
May we be bringers of your love.

We pray today for youth and young adults
of our church,
of our town,
and of our country and the whole world.
May we be encouragers
and supporters in hard times
and cheerleaders in good!

You are our God
and we are your people.

Thank you, God, thank you.

Amen.

1/29/12
1 Cor 8:1-13

We Pray Your Realm Comes Soon

Lord, the cold of winter is back!
We slip and slide and hope each of us stays safe.

Safe from bad weather
is one thing but safe from evil is another.

Lord, we despair of
ever finding peace!
We pray your realm comes soon!
Yet we know, too, that you can banish our
unclean thoughts and spirit
with a word right now.

May our prayers
include the weak and unseemly
trying to find warm shelter
on this cold day. We pray for
the Salvation Army, and all of the
agencies that try to help.

May our prayers
include the wider world
where, for too, too many,
violence and evil are part of daily life.
We pray for peace and hope for all
caught in violence and war.

May our prayers
include our congregation
trying to discern your will
for us. We pray for
guidance and hope!

Thank you, God, Thank you.

Amen.

2/1/15
Mark 1:21-28

Transfigured

God, we don't think about you
as much as we ought
for you are dazzling,
blinding us routinely with
your brilliance and power!

Like Peter, we mutter something,
usually simple
and really more about ourselves
than you.

Still, there is something-
something about you
that draws us to do
apparently foolish things.

We give up our own time
to help build homes through
Habitat for Humanity;
thank you for standing beside us
hammering home
a nail or assembling
needed home goods.

We share our money
through Week of Compassion
blanketing those who
are cold and lost.

We buy an extra can of soup or two
just to have around
when someone hungry shows up.

It is good that we are
here with you, Lord,
even when we least expect it,
you might just turn up.

Thank you, God, thank you.

Amen.

Transfiguration - 3/6/11
Matthew 17:1-9

Spring Season

A Time for Penitence and Joy

Tommy's Pain and Joy

If it was this time of year in Spencerville, it'd look a lot like it does right here. Of course, they didn't have as many cranes or geese migrate through but still, you could hear the doves in the morning, just like here. And the trees lining the two-lane blacktop road as you finally got to the edge of town looked a lot like Locust Street did in the old days, before the tornadoes, maybe like Division Street does now. It was one of those little towns that you just feel good driving into.

On the way in, one of the first places you'd pass would be Red's Auto Service and Texaco Station, an old red barn-like building just in front of the grove of pecan trees the Wilson family farmed. It opened into a nice village square with a small gazebo in the center and there on the northwest corner was the Buttermilk Café, the local meeting and gathering place, where much local gossip could be found.

Of course, time in a small town like Spencerville is a funny thing. While the Bank opened precisely at 9:00 in the morning, the Buttermilk Café opened anywhere between 6 and 6:30, depending on when Elvira decided to unlock the front door. That would be after Walt, the milkman, snuck in the back to deliver milk and get a fresh cup of coffee and maybe a word or two with Elvira. Bernie and Bernice Staunton always came in at 7:05 and sat at the far end of the counter while Vern and Wally and Ron would fill the booth by the cash register.

Somedays they'd all be gone by 8:15; somedays nearer to 10:15. No matter what time, it was the right time. So I wasn't surprised when Tommy asked me to meet him precisely at 9:20 on Good Friday; I was just surprised he showed up then!

He was smiling that big, goofy smile of his as he bounced in the door. Elvira hollered, "Hey friend!" and brought him a glass of orange juice and a white powdered donut. It makes my mouth pucker up just to think about that combination but clearly it was Tommy's regular selection and Elvira had it ready.

Tommy didn't say anything to me, just smiled and ate that donut, white powdered sugar dust floating hazily in the sunbeams. I don't know what it was but that simple smile always made me happy. Sort of like my uncle's great smile and cousin's friendly greeting each time I'd see them.

When he'd finished the donut and taken a deep swig of the juice, he sighed comfortably and said, "Isn't Easter amazing?"

Have I told you about Tommy's eyes? They were deep blue but not the same shade. Sort of like two cat's eye marbles that seem to be the same until you looked at them closely. And he had a really steady gaze like there was someone standing right behind you that only he could see. It was disconcerting and, between that and the smile, most people thought he was kind of simple minded and handicapped. He may have appeared such, but those eyes held much sorrow and pain.

As he slowly twirled the orange juice glass in his hands, he told me why Easter was special. It hadn't always been so. In fact, 12 years before, on another bright Easter weekend, at 9:20 in the morning of Good Friday, his twin sister, Ruth had died in a car crash as she was returning home from college. Tommy looked down before continuing. When he looked up, he had that smile of his and I began to wonder if maybe he really was a bit crazy! Then he told me the story.

He told me the world lost all its color that day. His faith in just about anything died with his sister. He felt cold and he was alone as their parents had died also. Sometimes we can take painful situations, sometimes we seem to go with the flow but then something comes along, out of the blue like Aunt Betty's and Uncle John's deaths, and it all just seems like too much and we shut down. Even tears seem to dry up and we just stop feeling. That's what Tommy said happened to him.

He stopped going to church, he stopped listening to his heart and started listening to the pain, the blackness inside of him and it took away his love. He moved a lot during those years and just got darker and darker. Easter comes in springtime and you'd think over the years that his mood would change, that he'd slowly get over it but he didn't. He started getting madder and madder at God, at Jesus; and the joy of Easter just made him angry. How dare God take his sister! Jesus loves me? What hogwash! he'd say. He couldn't deal with the pain of it all, so he covered it up with his anger. But the pain came up in the dark of the night and he'd cry. Long and hard, he'd cry. He'd cry out to God, "Why? Why? I loved my sister, what have you done with her?! I prayed to you; I went to church - why?"

And then he said that something happened to him. One night as he cried, he heard a voice. He said it was like a voice in his head. The voice said, "Why are you crying? Tommy, you mean more to me than all those other things...your sister means more to me than anything and I'll never leave her - or you."

Tommy laughed then and looked out the window. A cardinal was on the telephone pole, bright red against the blue spring sky, a day as beautiful as today. He looked at me with that big smile and the tears in my eyes ran down my cheek like his. We didn't say anything for a minute. Then he said, "I know it was Jesus, the real Jesus that still lives. Ruthie's with him and that makes all the difference in the world 'cause he's with me too. Easter's real for me every day but especially at 9:20 am on Good Friday, that's why I asked to meet you then. Jesus took the blackest day of my life and gave it back to me. I still miss Ruthie, but the darkness is gone. Forever." And then he smiled and drank down the rest of his orange juice in one gulp. He stood and said, "Happy Easter, Scott" and walked out into the bright day, a little jaunt to his step and an easy swing of his arms.

Just another Easter in Spencerville.

Obedience is as Obedience Does

God, obedience is
as obedience does.

But what if we could
do this thing that would be
beneficial, that would
help someone,
that would take care of our need
to feel in control.

Lord, lord, how we are tempted
to do just that
all in the name of
goodness and mercy and justice
as if we hold the key
to the kingdom.

But you didn't ask us
to hold that key, did you?
You asked us to love you
with everything we've got
and to love our neighbor
as our self.

Obedience is
as obedience does, God.

We do not live by bread alone.
feed us your word
that we may grow
closer to you.

We shouldn't put you
to the test; help us to
rest peacefully in your arms,
good shepherd.

We shouldn't serve
anyone or thing but you;
for you are our God
and we are your people.

Thank you, God, thank you!

Amen.

3/9/14
Matthew 4:1-11

Turning About

Jesus, we've been to the wilderness
and found temptation
right outside our door.
We've tried to find
easy ways but
they haven't worked so well.

The warming days of springtime
grace us with glorious sunsets
washing the sky clear.

We rejoice and praise God!

And then we think again.
These days of Lent
remind us that repentance
is a real turning about
and we long for the
spring rain to wash
the eyes of our hearts
so we can see clearly.

We see families struggling
to make a new start at Hope Harbor
and we share some of your
abundance with them.

We hear of friends and coworkers
being laid off and we
pray for them and
struggle to think of ways
we can help.

We read of arrests
of those here illegally
and we worry about the children
helpless and lonely.

Hard problems, God, these are
hard problems and
we pray for your Spirit
to guide us.

Lord, help us in our helplessness.

Amen.

3/15/09
John 2:13-22

Anything Can Happen at a Well

Anything can happen at a well.
You just might meet
the Christ.

Like our innermost self,
a well is deep and dark
and wet and slippery,
dangerous
as a word that wounds
a hurting soul.

Yet we, all,
must come to the well and,
anything can happen at a well.

What is it to be known?
our whole life,
each bit and piece
sad and sorry
or overflowing with false pride?

Shamed and disgraced,
we try to hide behind
bravado and feigned disregard
or lack of concern.
But Jesus knows
and offers living water
that purifies and overflows
making us as happy
as a room without a roof!

May this joy fill
our fellowship hall
as we make sack lunches
to fill hungry lunch eaters!

May this happiness
bathe the NE AIDS Project
Benefit concert
next Saturday as we raise monies
to help folks suffering with HIV/AIDS!

May this love
surround us and fill us,
making us dance to know
that we are loved
even as we are known
so, so intimately!

Thank you, God, thank you!

Amen.

3/23/14
John 4:5-42

We Confess

The cranes are restless
and the skies resound with their
song to you, O God.
You have written
such beautiful music
in their minds and hearts!

Your whisper
is like thunder
and we praise
Your Holy Name!

Oh wait, I just got
a text message...
You see God, how we
choose to listen to ourselves?

We confess that
our prayers are often
self-centered
when we should pray for the
lonely in our nursing homes
and the children
brushed aside and underneath
by families struggling
to even have
two meals a day.

We confess that
our prayers are often
parochial and local
when we should pray for
those all around our country and world
affected by tornadoes and storms
and wars and strife.

Bless the hygiene kits we send
to Church World Service;
we'll never know
who we helped and that's okay.

We confess that
our prayers are often
improbably insincere and trite;
and yet the Sand Hill cranes
still glide across the sky,
singing glory,
glory,
glory!

Thank you, God, thank you.

Amen.

3/25/12
Jeremiah 31:31-34; John 12:20-33

Deliverance from Blindness

Hosanna, hosanna in the highest!
That's our cry, this day, Lord.
You ride into Jerusalem
and we so want you
to be 'King of Israel'
not understanding
you will not be our new 'David'.

Hosanna, hosanna in the highest!
Again we sing it out
and the crowd chants and sways
in the promise they think you hold.

The crowds will change as the week goes on
and the fact that you aren't king David
becomes clearer.

I fear it wasn't hard
for the chief Priests
to sway the crowds,
to suggest Barabas,
to insist on death.

This morning, we pray
for deliverance from our blindness.
Show us the way to everlasting life
even as it challenges us today
as much as it did in your day, Lord Jesus.

This morning, we pray
for those suffering illness and sorrow.
May they be restored to good health and home.

This morning, we pray
for our community,
for our leaders. May they find
renewed spirits to extend
grace and mercy to all our citizens
within our wide community.

Thank you, God, Thank you.

Amen.

Palm Sunday - 3/29/15
John 12:12-16

How Many Times Must I Tell You?

Amazing! I was blind
but now I see!

Now hold on, hold on,
was it done correctly?
Were the proper permits
pertaining to the restoration
of sight obtained?

And were doctors' affidavits
provided to support
the claim of blindness?

You realize, of course,
that this permit for sight
is only good Monday to Saturday,
Sunday won't do; not at all.

How many times must I tell you?
I was blind
but now I see! Amazing!

God, what light is this that
floods our spirits and frees us
to truly love you
and our neighbor?
It is the light of the world, indeed!

Light up our hearts, God,
as we celebrate our
successful Relay for Life fund raiser.
Your blessings filled us
as we worked.

Light up our imaginations, Lord,
as we struggle to see
with your light rather
than our own. Fill our
prayers with praise!

Light up our souls, Eternal Creator,
guide us to do
your will each day.

Thank you, God, thank you!

Amen.

3/30/14
John 9:1-41

Peace Be with You

God, O God, Jesus has died!
But Mary tells us she's
seen him, talked to him.
Her face, streaked
with the tears of sorrow
and pain, beamed
at the sound of
her name.

Lord, is it you?
How?
Why?
Did I not tell you
I must suffer and die
and then rise again?

It is so; peace be with you;
now - go tell the others.

New life looks
almost unrecognizable
when set against
the blackness of
fear and distrust and anger.
Is it true as the scriptures say
that something must die
for new life to appear?

Then let our greed die, Lord!
Open the eyes of our hearts
to see needs we can fulfill.

Let our privilege and power die, Creator!
The feet of so many
need washing, need caring, need loving.

Let our fear and anger die, Mother Mary!
Help us to let that which
holds us back, die.
That which ties us to a darkness
near to death, die.
It is truly in the resurrection
that we, too, are offered
new life,
new hope;
Joy!

He is risen!

Thank you, God, thank you.

Amen.

Easter - 3/31/13
John 20:1-18

Your Light Will Show

This morning, of all mornings, God
rushing to get to church
rushing to find the shoe,
the necktie, the car keys,
rushing, rushing...

left just enough time to see
the sunrise.

We were blind but now
we see.

Like the Pharisees of old,
we know what we know,
indeed, we believe we know everything!

Only we don't; there is much
for us to see that only
your light will show.

How can we see the plight
of the poor and needy
without your light
shining over the far side of the tracks,
way back in the underpass?

How can we see the needs
of the children
unless your light shines
down low enough to
get around our high-brow
ideas and concerns?

How can we see the elderly
except with your
light that shines and guides
us through our darkest days?

We pray thank you, Lord,
for the still, steady light
that helps us to see
peace and beauty and hope.

Thank you, God, thank you.

Amen.

4/3/11
John 9:1-41

I Wouldn't Recognize You

Somedays, God, I am so busy,
I wouldn't recognize you if
you were standing right next to me!

I wouldn't recognize you if
you were standing there at the bus stop
shivering in the cold because
you didn't have a warm coat.

I wouldn't recognize you slowly
pushing a half empty shopping cart
down the aisle at the supermarket,
searching
for specials and bargains, as I zipped
around you to grab some tea.

When will I slow down

take a deep, clean breath

and

offer you a smile?

You, who have given such an
abundant invitation to life.
You, who loves us
even when we behave unlovably.

The emptiness we sometimes feel
and always try to cover up
with things and distractions
is where we'll mostly find you, isn't it?

The grass is turning greener and
the nights are less chilly - your
creation is awakening in a burst
of new life.

That deep, clean breath feels good.

It is good to smile, to invite another
to refresh themselves in your presence.

Thank you, God. May your love
and compassion bless us always.

Amen.

4/6/08
Luke 24:13-35

In the Worrying

It's true, isn't it, God?

We want the garden but
we want to eat the forbidden fruit too.
We want to have what we
don't have;
We want to throw away what we
do have.

The trees of spring tease us
with small lights of green
budding forth as if to say
"it's spring!" in the midst
of a snowstorm.

What a journey we're on!
Did Abraham and Sarah worry
as much as we do?
Did Moses give up worrying
after you said, "That's it - you're
going to Egypt?"

How long it takes us to recognize that
You are in both the worrying
and the going.

Lord God, there are those among us
suffering from health issues and
we pray for them; we pray for healing
trusting in you to know
what healing is best.

Mother God, we pray always for the
children. We pray for safety for
those suffering in broken families.
Give parents patience and strength

to love their children in spite
of their own problems.

Creator God, you are our hope
in a world crying out for hope.
We pray for peace; we pray for
your guidance to help us
stop the violence which only
breeds more violence.

God - Thy will be done,
in the worrying
and the going forth.

Amen.

4/13/08
John 10:1-10

Suddenly

Easter sunrise bright
You suddenly appear,
You suddenly appear.

The tomb is empty and cold
death warmed over yearns
for the warming sunlight
but is forever locked in the tomb.

We stand as frozen by the angel's
words as the two Marys, frozen in fear
yet dazzled at the same time!

God, we were so scared that
you were gone, that all our stories
would begin with 'do you remember when'
and then
You suddenly appear,
You suddenly appear.

Lord, we know we have
problems right here in our town,
problems with hunger and homelessness,
problems with unemployment and hopelessness.

But You suddenly appear
as a friend working at a Habitat home,
as a handshake at Salvation Army,
in a shared moment at a local
nursing home or retirement community.

You suddenly appear
when we come together in worship
filling our cups,
restoring our souls.

You suddenly appear
when we least expect it,
surrounded by fear
that we might be alone.
Then - You suddenly appear.

Thank you, God, thank you.

Amen.

Easter - 4/24/11
Matthew 28:1-10

Stewardship is a Gift

The breath of God stilled the waters
of creation,
smoothing them and blessing them.
The breath of God
gave life to the dust
from which we came,
the breath of God is our
counselor and advocate today.

There is a peacefulness
that we share
with all creation. It is the peace
of being a part of
all
that is.

Our stewardship was never intended
as a burden but rather
a participation with
the trees that bend to the wind,
the grass, green with new life,
the birds migrating to the
ancient pulse of it all.

We understand your call, God,
as we clean the shoreline
of L. E. Ray lake,

As we collect aluminum cans
to recycle for Habitat for Humanity,

As we work at Kamp Kaleo to
repair and prepare for your children
to come play and learn and grow,
we understand your call.

Stewardship is a gift; it is a blessing
you bestow.

Help us to be your servants, God,
help us to open our hearts to all of your
ongoing creation.

Today - earth stewardship Sunday - we pray
for all those who work for the environment,
but perhaps we pray most for our own eyes
and hearts to be open
to the needs right here
in our community.

Thank you, God. Jesus promised
he would not leave us orphaned;
in your life-giving breath,
we are loved.

Amen.

4/27/08
John 14:15-21

Your Spirit at Work

Lord, there is little
to differentiate us anymore.
We eat the same foods,
we watch the same TV,
we scan the same Facebook.

On the other hand,
we fragment so easily -
republican or democrat,
liberal or conservative,
husker or Jayhawk...
we look at ourselves
rather than You.

Long ago, Peter
witnessed your Spirit
at work in the very ones
he knew were outside,
stranger, godless.

Would that we, too,
may listen and see your
presence and love in the
least likely places and people.

For You are still speaking,
still creating
and we are today's witnesses,
the hands and heart of Christ
for the world to know,
a movement for wholeness
in a fragmented world.

We are the hands
that build Habitat houses
and repair Kamp Kaleo.
We are the smiles and greetings

that welcome visitors
and neighbors to our Garden Walk
and Festival of the Booths ministries.
We are the hosts
that hold a place for
everyone at the table.

Thank you, God, thank you.

Amen.

4/28/13
Acts 11:1-18

A Surprising God

"My God, my God, why have you
forsaken me?" the psalmist cries in Psalm 22.
We know this feeling, God.

If you are here
even in the midst of our suffering,
show yourself! Show us
how to be the people
you have made us to be.

The psalmist knew, too,
how you are within and
without nature,
nurturing us like the
flowers of the field,
like a daisy waiting patiently
for the sun.

The most surprising thing, God,
is that our enemies know
you this way too!

You are a surprising God,
aren't you?

Just when we think
we have you all figured out,
you turn the tables
inviting all-
even us - with our notions
of who belongs and who doesn't!

Help us to find your simplicity,
your easy way with the world,
in the work that we do
preparing for the Nebraska State Fair,
in the faces of strangers
we'll meet there.

Help us to be your simplicity
serving meals at Salvation Army.

Help us to widen our reach
for you.

Thank you, God, thank you.

Amen.

5/2/10
Acts 11:1-18

for Our Sins are Great

O Lord, we so often
take charge in place
of you.
Actions and words
demeaning the very
people you love,
we make you out
to be a liar and a fraud.

Forgive us, Father,
for our sins are great.

Dear God, we never
think our piety
to be false bravado
yet our plowshares
have become swords
all too often.

Forgive us, Mother,
for our sins are great.

Jesus, you came not
to speak your words but
to testify to God's words.
We thank you and pray for
understanding and hope.
We pray today for children
lost in the cracks of a torn world.
Help us to minister to children
whenever we can. Bless the
teddy bears and stuffed animals
we donate to the Police and Firemen.

We pray today for the elderly and sick,
left lonely at home and in nursing homes.
Give us persistence to maintain
contact with our shut-in members.

We pray today for this year's graduates.
Keep them safe as they drive
distracted by parties and celebrations.

Thank you, God, thank you.

Amen.

5/20/12
1 John 5:9-13, John 17:6-19

Re-collected

God of remembering,
in you, all endings are really
beginnings since
You are the end without end.

The end of Jesus' baptism was
the beginning of his ministry.
The end of his journey to Jerusalem
was the beginning of your glorification.

The end of his crucifixion was
the beginning of your amazing
act of resurrection!

As Noah watched the rains and storms
swirling around, bringing an end
to the world, it was just
the beginning with
a dove and an olive branch.

We need to be re-membered,
re-collected, re-joined.

We live in a world
that is never as safe and sure as
we try to make ourselves
believe it is.

Storms and earthquakes
happen. And we, soaked and homeless,
struggle to understand.

O God give us strength in the face
of overwhelming need,
give us hope so that we can
meet the challenges of helping
the victims of the cyclone in Myanmar,
of the earthquake in China.

But help us also, God, to see
the needs right here at home, too.

Just as Abraham didn't let the legions
of promised sand grains
blind him to the strangers at Mamre,
so may we not be blinded by
our illusions of wealth and peace;
it is not so for everyone
here in Grand Island, NE.

Yet Jesus said, "And remember, I am with you always."

Today, we are once again
re-membered with and in you.

Thank you, God, thank you.

Amen.

5/18/08
Matt 28:16-20

Mother to Us All

Mother God, we praise you
this day by honoring mothers.
And women who aren't mothers,
and women who don't want to be mothers
and women who are but not so good.

Father God, we praise you
this day by honoring all women
for all are beloved of God.

Creator, you have blessed us
with life abundant
and you came among us
to show us the way
to such a life;
salvation lived daily
with joy and peace
amidst the pain and suffering
of this world.

You give us serenity
to accept the things we cannot
change,
courage to change the
things we can, and the wisdom
to know the difference.

Eternal Light, we pray for our nation,
that we might be humble enough
to listen and strong enough
to accept when we are wrong.

Sophia Wisdom, we pray
for our church.
May we be an oasis
to renew and rejuvenate
all of us for your mission.

Holy God, we pray
with thanks for your
guidance and grace.
We know You are doing
new things and we shout with joy
to know you better, to share our story
more fervently;
even though the road ahead
may be filled with potholes
and unknown twists and turns,
we fear no evil or suffering
as it brings us closer to You.

Thank you, God, thank you.

Amen.

5/12/13
Acts 16:16-34

Change Is Hard, Lord

Light of all light,
we so enjoy doing things
the way we've always done them!
Of course, that really means
this is the way we've done them
since the last time we changed.
Which no one can
remember when.

Change is hard, Lord.

In fact, we'll settle for
sickness and handicaps
just so we don't have to change.

As B'rer Rabbit might've said,
"You can make me do this
or do that, but whatever you do,
don' make me change!"

Wellness does indeed have a cost.

Creator, we pray today
for those living
on the edge.
Whether it's healthcare
or transportation or just
getting a day's meal,
remind us to support Agape`, and the Lighthouse,
and Cityride Circuit and
all the agencies that
bridge the gaps in someone's
green pastures.

Lord Jesus, we pray today
for those in our congregation
suffering loss and illness.

Be with them; may your mercy and grace
give them peace and hope.

Dearest Holy Spirit, we pray today
for our church. Small as we are,
we need your guidance and direction.
We pray especially for our Search Committee;
help us to let them know they
have our support and trust.

Thank you, God, Thank you.

Amen.

5/1/16
John 5:1-9

Just One Spirit

Like a dove come down
from Heaven, Holy Spirit
descends upon us
giving us priceless gifts -
wisdom and understanding,
counsel and might,
knowledge and fear of the Lord.

Help us to know that while
this gift takes many forms,
there is just one Spirit,
a movement of God -
a bridge building, barrier breaking
movement of God!

Be with us this day, Creator.
Be with us as we pray
for healing and hope for those
in hospital and at home
recovering from illness.

Be with us this day, Lord Jesus.
Be with us as we pray
for the least of these in our community.
Help us and guide us to feed and clothe,
visit and nurse, all in need.

Be with us this day, Holy Spirit.
Be with us as we pray
for our search committee.
Guide them in their effort and deliberation.
Nurture those looking for calls
that the one you guide
hears your call on our behalf.

Thank you, God, thank you!

Amen.
Pentecost - 5/15/16 | Acts 2:1-21

In Memoriam

We stand here with heads bowed,
silent
with respect and honor
for those fallen in war and conflict.

We know that your way is peace;
forgive us for our violence.

But our friends, oh God,
and our family have died
defending us and sustaining us
and we mourn their loss.

But you are ever with us,
whether as footprints in the sand
or a calming feeling
deep in our souls.

Let us rest a moment in your peace.

[*observe 1-2 minutes of silence*]

Thank you, God, thank you!

Amen.

Memorial Day - 5/25/14
John 14:15-24

Summer Season

A Time for Service and Love

Tommy and Change

I pulled into Spencerville and found a parking space in front of the Buttermilk Café. The Town Square was full of summer with birds singing and sunlight splashing. But I was so caught up in my problems and worries, I only noticed the birds because one pooped on my windshield! Later I noticed the green leaves and sunlight. Later - after coffee with Tommy. It was just after 10 in the morning and the Café wasn't too busy. Most of the normal customers had finished their coffee and headed out for the day's work. But Tommy was still there at the corner of the counter and Elvira was just bringing him a cup of coffee - I guess he'd just come in.

I said, "Hi Tommy - got room?"

"Sure."

Elvira brought me a cup of coffee too and offered a menu which I impatiently waved off. Now I need to tell you that Tommy is a good listener, probably one of the best I've ever met. He puts his whole self into it. He never gets his phone out; he never interrupts. Somehow, he looks like the only and most important thing in the world at that immediate moment is to listen to me. Whenever I listen well, it's because I'm trying to listen like Tommy.

This day, my worry and irritation was taxes. Yes, taxes! I'd gotten a letter from the IRS regarding my taxes from a few years back. Here it is a week later, and I still haven't dealt with it - been putting it off as though maybe it would go away. I knew better from past experience, but old ways are hard to change.

"Tommy, I got a letter from the IRS. They claim I owe nearly $1500 more in taxes for 2014! They claim the Pension Fund reported $49,500 in distribution! It was my savings account, not an investment!!" I spilled out in one big run-on sentence.

"Oh no!" Tommy said.

I looked at him, but he didn't say anything, just kept listening. "What am I going to do?"

Tommy said, "I don't know - what are you going to do?"

This gave me free rein to pontificate on the evil IRS, the incompetent Pension Fund and let's throw in the Post Office just for the heck of it. They're all out to make my life miserable. If they'd just get their act together, I wouldn't have these problems. Tommy said, "Yes, but what are you going to do?" Isn't it a pain how someone who's a good listener doesn't get sidetracked?

I paused and said, "I guess I'll call the pension fund first. I sure don't want to call the IRS!"

"That sounds like a good thing." Tommy replied.

I paused and caught my breath. "Tommy, why do I procrastinate and put stuff off so much? Do you have trouble with putting off stuff or feeling like they're out to get you?"

Tommy did that thing he does when he's thinking - he looks at you but he's not looking at you. He sort of looks over your shoulder like there's something important somewhere. It's disconcerting but I'm used to it now.

"Well" he said. "Nothing to it but to do it!"

That rang in my head with its simplicity and rhymey sound, "nothing to it but to do it." As I took that in, it seemed to me that I'd spent a whole lot of years avoiding and putting off things just because I wasn't able 'to do it' so to speak.

"Tommy, why is it so hard for me to change the way I do things?"

"Because, in order to change - you have to change."

Slowly, the coffee receded from our cups as the weight of that simple admonition sank in. I chuckled and mentioned I had a phone call to make. We said our goodbyes and headed for the door, waving goodbye to Elvira and hello to prudent change!

Forgive Our Foolishness

O God, the waters are rising.
Our very lives seem in peril,
all hope seems lost.

We long to walk with you, God
as Noah walked with you;
we long to ride in the
deeps of your ark of safety.

Yet we hold onto our illusions,
dreams of grandeur and glory
from victorious battles,
all the while telling ourselves
it's okay to be violent
in a good cause.

Forgive our foolishness.

Creator, peel back our illusion
that this is a land of wealth;
for there are children who
will go hungry this morning.

Mother, fling off our shroud
of complacency that keeps
folks in nursing homes and
hospitals alone and lonely.

Father, don't laugh at our
feigned weakness in the face of
needs all over our community,
but give us strength to
find ways to help our neighbors
in Kearney and Aurora
where tornadoes struck this week.

Above all, God, give us your peace
that surpasses understanding
and illusion.

Thy will be done
is
our greatest peace.

Thank you, God, thank you.

Amen.

6/1/08
Genesis 6:9-22; 7:24; 8:14-19

We Praise You, God

God of eternity, our God—
we are your people
and it astounds us that you
are zealous for us!

Hot with energy enough
to still the raging storms of chaos,
you sit with children
gently laughing.

Flush with a love we cannot deny
you weep when we weep;
you ache when we ache;
you won't even leave us
when we die.

So we praise you God!

We praise you in the aisle
at Walmart, we praise you
under sunny clouds
amid smoke of grilled
burgers and chicken,
we praise you with our
arms around children
happy to be our readers.

We praise you with the sound
of ringing hammers,
with the rustle of sewing shears
and the rip of saws,
we praise you with the deliberation
of councils and the fears
of uncertainty
in which you are our only rock.

We praise you now, in silence, too.

[*brief silence*]

Remember our soldiers,
our forest fighters, our highway patrols;
remember our nurses and doctors
and our ministers all over
your good creation.

Thank you, God, thank you.

Amen.

6/6/10
Galatians 1:11-24

The Sound of the Wind

The sound of the wind
echoes from so long ago,
tongues of flame and voices
speaking in tongues of understanding
between strangers on this day,
this Pentecost.

Forgive us, Lord, if we have doubted
in angry grudges and perverse revenge.
Forgive us as we forgive those
we wish to blame and hurt back.

It does no one any good
and, if you choose anything forever,
You choose life.

Unforgiveness will be the death of us,
dead to your life abundant
and dead to the Spirit
rushing around and through us
today and always.

Breathing in and out,
prayers, simple prayers
easily fill us, whispering
Lord, let your light
come into my heart;

Lord, have mercy on me,
a sinner;
Lord, open my lips
and my mouth will proclaim your praise.

Creator, your breath
gave life to simple dust.
This week, we have breathed
your life into Garden Walk fellowship,
cheese puff heads,
and new life in baptism!
Thank you, God,
In praise, we thank you!

Amen.

Pentecost - 6/12/11
John 20:19-23

For the Times He Was Bold

Father, on this Father's Day
we're not sure what to say.
Thank you, Dad?
We love you, Dad?

Maybe that and much more
for fathers who've cared
for us.

Maybe we say 'thank you, dad'
for the times he was bold
and seemed fearless and strong.
Strong enough to fend off
all our fears
of the monsters under beds
and lurking in closets.

Strong enough to take
our youthful put downs
when we thought
we knew best
but didn't really know anything.

Gentle enough to hold us
as we cried over that
lost love or our
broken down car.
It is this strength
and fearlessness that we now see
was only there through faith;
Our doubts and fears
shackle us too and we marvel
that you ever survived our nonsense!

Thank you, dad, we love you.

Thank you for the men
who showed us that prayer
wasn't just for wimps
but prayed best by the strong
who know their limitations.

Thank you for the men
who loved us unconditionally,
whose patient presence
reflected stamina and endurance.

Thank you for the men
who paid no attention to convention
loving us because they could
even while wearing silly costumes!

Thank you, God, thank you!

Amen.

Father's Day - 6/15/14
Acts 3:1-10; 4:1-21

You Do Not Fit Well into Boxes

Your Son said, "Father, forgive them,
they know not what they do."
Is it true that
You are forgiving?
Or rather like a distant father
who is an unknown
except for the occasional
birthday or holiday
or Easter Sunday morning?

And what are we as Your children?
Do we say we'll work
only to blow it off
or do we leave you
without a word of goodbye or care
like the boy Jesus?

You do not fit well
into boxes, God, and images
are only that -
not the real thing.

But no matter how we describe you,
You are there.
Wanting a relationship,
not caring if we forget to send a card,
indifferent to the gift of another tie.
It is simply us
that You desire.

Then bless us, Father;
bless our new Oasis service.
May it refresh and renew
us to go out and work
in your vineyard.

Yes, bless us, Lord;
bless our new roof
and all the people we will
grace with your hospitality.

Bless us, most mysterious Creator,
with hope and strength
for the kingdom and glory
are yours,
forever and ever.

Thank you, God, thank you.

Amen.

6/16/13
Matthew 21:28-32; Luke 2:41-51

Salt and Light

God, it's dark in here
sometimes. It feels like
I'm all alone.
But when the light is
barely enough to
make a shadow,
I feel better.

You light up my world, Lord.

And when my fries
come with no seasoning
and a curse tries to
escape my lips,
I know the blessing of salt
stinging as it purifies.

You salt my thought, Creator.

When we are most
in your image,
we are salt and light
for the world!

Today, we pray for our world.
As peoples move and shift,
we grow fearful; help us
to welcome the stranger
for we were strangers once, too.

Today we pray for our community.
Bless us with service
and commitment to support
Agape, Concern, Eldercare
and so many other outreach efforts.

Today we pray for our congregation.
Guide us on our search for
a new minister. Hear our prayers
for strength, discernment and patience.

Thank you, God, Thank you.

Amen.

6/26/16
Matthew 5:13-16

A Call of Creation

What Lord? Did you call?
Did you leave me a voicemail
or a text message
calling my attention to you?

Sun and moon, wind and rain,
each a call upon our souls,
a call of creation, a call of identity.

Whisper to us, Jesus,
like the whisper of the snow on an uncovered cheek
or the brush of light from a beam of spring.

The intensity of the light
that comes from nowhere
and everywhere at once,
blinds us to everything but you.

And we open our eyes to see anew.
You have revealed yourself
to us once more!

We pray for the willingness
to listen to your call, Lord.

Thank you, God, thank you!

Amen.

6/29/14
Acts 9:1-25

But You're Not

God, sometimes, when I'm angry
or particularly self-absorbed,
I can make myself believe
that you're angry at the
same people I am.

But you're not.

Sometimes, we can feel
like you're especially
on our side, God.

But you're not.

And sometimes, God, we think
we're making big sacrifices for you
but we're really making them
for ourselves, aren't we?

This morning, the sun shines
and does not wonder if it is good.
This morning, like Abraham,
we arose through the mists,
driving through growing cornfields,
purposed with love for you, God.

So we pray for your help
as we begin the final
preparation to go help tornado recovery
in Greensburg, KS.
Help us realize that
you will provide
the patience, the love, the strength
to do what we need to do
to be a help rather than a hindrance.

We pray for your compassion
as we mourn and worry
about our friends and family
suffering illness and pain and loss.

We pray for courage
to move beyond ourselves,
to that thin space where
You work best.

Sometimes, God, we feel
like you're far away,

but you're not.

Thank you, God, thank you.

Amen.

6/29/08
Genesis 22:1-14

What if Everyone Repents?

O God, my God
how majestic is your creation!

But some days, Tarshish sounds like
a good choice, God.
You have sent us
yet we demur, sure
that it's going to turn
out badly.

What if we do as you ask,
be the tillers and keepers
of paradise?
What if everyone repents?

You are a just
and merciful God,
eager for reconciliation.

Like a gigantic fish,
Nineveh might swallow
us up whole and spit us out
wet and cold on a clear, sandy beach.

We will pray today
with reverence
as we celebrate
Independence Day.
Prayers for those in our military
unable to be at home
with their loved ones.
May we all pray for peace.

We will pray today
for those suffering loss and sorrow.
Be with all in need.

We will pray today
for those sick and ill;
bring your healing grace
in abundance!

Thank you, God, Thank you.

Amen.

7/5/15
Jonah 1:1-3a; 17-2:6

Set Us Free

Sometimes, God, it seems
like it's all we can do just to stay in place!

All around us are sharks and hidden agendas;
even the safety of our homes
can seem threatened.

Set us free, Lord, set us free!

In Your kindom,
there is no longer one or another but both and.
The walls we use to separate us
crumble and all are set free.

We pray for your guidance, Creator.
Lead us into your light and life.

We pray for your strength, Eternal Light
that we may be a light of love
in our community activities.

We pray for your peace, Holy Spirit,
that our witness to our world
is one of unity and welcome to all!

Thank you, God, thank you!

Amen.

7/6/14
Galatians 3:25-28, 5:1

O Lord, Hear Our Prayers

O God, there is a darkness
that descends even in the light of day.
It squeezes our hearts;
it makes the pit
of our stomachs drop.

We're scared and hurt
and not sure we can bear
our sorrow, Lord;
that's where we're at.

Like Rachel weeping in Ramah,
we cry for those who died or were wounded
wherever violence explodes.
We cry for those suffering now
and for those afraid for their future.

O Lord, Hear our prayers.

We pray for the dead.
We cannot un-shoot them.
We pray for their loved ones,
for their consolation:
"Blessed are those who mourn,
for they will be comforted."

We pray for the living.
We pray for those who
seek dialogue, and an end
to violence and hatred.
"Blessed are the peacemakers,
for they will be called children of God."

We pray for protestors and police.
They will be misunderstood
and placed in harm's way
for the sake of others.

"Blessed are those who are persecuted
for righteousness' sake,
for theirs is the kingdom of heaven."

O Lord, Hear our prayers.

Thank you, God, Thank you.

Amen.

7/10/16
Matthew 5:21-26

Another Day

Another day, another
day, O God.

We get up; we break our fast
and wash our face,
we read the morning paper
and brush our teeth.

Thank you, God, thank you.

The dishes sit quietly
in the sink; they will
wait patiently all day for our return.
Our children play all day,
too excited to care
about kitchen cleanliness!

Thank you, God, thank you.

Vacation Bible School starts this week;
who will drive on which day
and who will provide
meals that nourish and please?
Who will teach and who will pray?

Thank you, God, thank you.

Birthdays will be celebrated
and this week, someone will cry;
someone will feel all alone and
someone will receive a special call
of friendship and concern; elders
will ponder what it means
to be a shepherd.

Thank you, God, thank you.

The phone will still ring...
and the calendar will fill...
each and every encounter
offering an opportunity
for hope and joy and love.

[*pause*]

Thank you, God, thank you.

Amen.

7/11/10
Colossians 1:1-14

As You Promised

God, you say such outlandish
things that we laugh
in disbelief.
And yet, you do as you promised.

Into the fear and cynicism
of our disbelief,
you breathe life
that disregards social
convention,
saving the one cast out
and rewarding the barren.

The storytellers
whisper and they shout
reminding us that you are
as much a part of our story
as we are.
At the heart of our plot,
we find you.

We pray today
for the people of Israel and Palestine.
May they find some way
beyond war and violence
to resolve their disagreements.

We pray today
for the lost and lonely children
who have come to our country.
Help and guide us to treat them
the way we would like our children
to be treated.

We pray today
for our church and our congregation.
Help us to know your love and strength
as we struggle to be your people.
Guide us always; thy will be done.

Thank you, God, thank you!

Amen.

7/13/14
Genesis 16:1-4, 18:9-15, 21:1-19

Pray for Us Sinners

God, have you seen
the Internet? There's sex
all over the place!
Ask a simple question
you might get a dirty answer.

And no one even
has to know.

How selfish can we be?!
Buried in a glowing
screen, we can live out
our wildest fantasies
all the while thinking
we're hurting no one.

What a charade
of self-satisfaction
we weave stifling out
what you made good!

Pray for us sinners,
now and at the hour of our death!

So we pray today for our world
given over to sinful pleasures.
Help us to be community for each other,
lifting up whatsoever is pure,
closer to Your heart, God,
so that we can see each other
as humans and not objects.

We pray today for our community,
for those who are hungry
and looking for work.
Help us to be ready
to lend a hand wherever we can.

We pray today for our church
and search committee.
Give us strength and patience.
guide our next minister
to our welcome!

Thank you, God, Thank you.

Amen.

7/17/16
Matthew 5:27-32

Blind Like Jesus

God, you see all that we
are capable of, don't you?
Doesn't matter what society says,
what the cultural norms say,
what we say about each other.

We say, 'prostitute', 'criminal',
'Liar' and on and on
then you say
'friend', 'dinner partner',
'builder of nations'...
'child of God'.

You see beyond
the limits we feel
and the ceilings and boundaries
we erect.

Blind to our perception, Jesus,
you never notice
the categories we damn each other with.
Would that we could be
blind like Jesus, too.

We pray with sincerity
for peace. Airplanes shot
from the sky, babies pulled
from the rubble of bombs,
Such havoc and suffering
have no kin with your love.

We pray with humility
for grace and guidance.
Help us to 'Be the Church'
at our Faith in Action Sunday
in September.

We pray with joy
for friendship and love.
Help us to share your joy
that knows no end.

Thank you, God, thank you!

Amen.

7/20/14
Joshua 2:1-21; 6:22-25

Go and Do Likewise

It would seem almost
obvious 'who our neighbor' is
yet we carry around
a load of baggage that
separates us through fear and doubt.

Walking down the sidewalk,
through a back alley,
driving to Walmart,
parking to walk by the greeter-
Who is my neighbor?

Jesus says the one who is
the neighbor is the one
who shows mercy
to the scary and time-consuming
other who looks nothing
like 'us'.

'Go and do likewise', You say, Jesus.
Go and do likewise.

Lord, teach us to pray
for we don't always
know how, don't always
have the strength
to go and do likewise!

Teach us to pray
for the child who can't read;
strengthen us to be their
reading buddies.

Teach us to pray
for the retiree
who has lost a few steps
and sees their world

through darker eyes;
let us be the light
that brightens their world today.

Teach us to pray
so we learn how to
go and do likewise--

Teach us to pray
Thy will be done on earth
as it is in heaven.

Thank you, God, thank you.

Amen.

7/21/13
Luke 10:25-37

Thin Space

There is a thin space
between heaven and earth;
there's a thin space between
hell and earth, too.

We push and strain at these
boundaries, unsure where
to turn, too sure
of our own way
or the way of the moment!

God, we want to stick you
in one place or the other
never quite noticing
that you are
the
thin
space...

If we might just trust
in that, if we might
find the strength of obedience
in that,
thin
becomes quite wide enough
for you - and us.

Jacob laid his head
on the thin space,
astounded to find you there,
almost like our surprise at
finding you wearing an apron
at Salvation Army or taking out
the trash at Hope Harbor!

Help us, God, be patient
with our maneuvers and hedges,
destined to put us
on one side
or the other.

Thin space us today,
and always.

Thank you, God, thank you.

Amen.

7/25/10
Colossians 2:6-15

Who Is Our Neighbor?

Jesus, the lawyer asked you
a question -
you didn't answer it
but looked at us
from a point of view
we never expected.

Mostly, we'd just like
the simple answer, please.

Who is our neighbor?

It's like worrying over
who ate the last potato chip
or who snores the loudest
or any other of a long list
of suitcases and satchels and handbags
that we cling to make us
feel justified in doing what
we wanted to do in the first place.

Maybe the question is
can we show mercy?
What must we let go of
to let mercy come first?

Whatever it is,
Jesus tells us to
'Go and do likewise'.

So let us go and do likewise
when we help with siding
on a Habitat House
or clean the gutters
of someone who can't do it themselves.

Let us go and do likewise
when we take the time
to greet someone strange to us.

Let us go and do likewise
when we find
the ways we can
partner with God
in God's redemptive mission
in the world.

Thank you, God, thank you.

Amen.

7/28/13
Luke 10:25-37

Help Us to See

Dear Lord, your patience
is legendary, and ours,
well, less so.

David's impatient desire
is before us
and we are shocked
and disappointed by
his rape and abuse
of Bathsheba and her husband, Uriah.

No more disappointed than you, God,
aware and angered
at David's lust.

Nathan tells a story
and David indicts himself
even as his blindness
needed Nathan's "You are the man!"
exclamation to be cured.

Dear Lord, help us to see
what we're blind to,
our short sight and self-interest.
We pray for your guidance.

Eternal Light, help us to see
those needs in our community
that we can fulfill as we
go out and 'be the church'
on Faith in Action' Sunday.
We pray for your guidance.

Holy Wisdom, help us to see
anew the face of a stranger
who may well be Christ,
hungry or afraid and alone.
We pray for your guidance.

Thank you, God, thank you!

Amen.

8/3/14
2 Samuel 11:1-5

Think About Today

Creator, we're worried
about tomorrow.
Will we have enough
food?
safety?
life?

But tomorrow isn't even here yet.

And if there are people
hungry today,
you would have us feed them, right?
And if there are people
alone today,
you would have us visit them, right?

We confess, God, that
many times, we aren't even
thinking about today.

Help us to think about today
and how our little pantry
helps feed someone.

Help us to think about today
and how our work on
Worship and Wonder children's church
helps teach and embrace a child.
Help us to think about today
and how our hospitality
to the stranger may be
just the right food to nourish
their spirit and heart.

Tomorrow isn't here yet;
thank goodness we only have to
live today!

Thank you, God, thank you.

Amen.

8/4/13
Luke 12:13-21

The Water is a Scary Place

The water is a scary place;
you can drown in it
or maybe even be reborn
but whatever happens,
the water is a scary place.

It is a place of storms and hurricanes
tsunamis, typhoons
terrible winds sweeping us
out of the safety of our boat.

Then you walk into our lives
and the wind ceases.

Thank you, God, thank you.

Thank you today for the
gardeners and workers
who struggle against the
growing grass - and weeds!

Thank you today for the
church universal of which
we are but a part, separate pieces
making a whole larger
than its sum.

Thank you today for the
gift of your grace given to us
in baptism and revealed
at your table through
your Son-
our friend and savior, Jesus.

The water is a scary place
but whatever happens
You
are with us.

Thank you, God, thank you.

Amen.

8/7/11
Matthew 14:22-33

Kernels of Hope

God, in the darkness
as sorrow surrounds us
over the loss of loved ones,
it's hard to know what to hang on to.
But maybe you
are the best we can hope for.

We cry like Orpah and Ruth and Naomi,
hesitant to separate;
unsure where to go next.

Ruth models loyalty for us:
Your people shall be my people;
your God shall be my God.

Doesn't make things easier
but softens the sorrow
enough to glean the kernels
of hope from the threshing floor.

Our prayers reach to you, Creator,
for the hope of the future.
Bless our missions with workers
and satisfaction!

Our prayers reach to you, Lord
for guidance and blessing.
Encourage us to share you
through our lives;
use words if we have to!

Our prayers reach to you, Abba
for peace wherever there is strife,
for outrage at atrocities,
for strength to go on
asking and planning and striving
for peace!

Thank you, God, thank you!

Amen.

8/10/14
Ruth 1:1-17a

And the World was Fed

A little boy asked his mom,
"Can I go out with everyone to see Jesus?"
She said yes, and packed him lunch-
5 small barley loaves and 2 fish.
"You can share with your friends
if you need to," she said.

When the Master asked his disciples
what they had to feed everyone,
the little boy said,
"Here - mom
said I could share these."

And the world was fed.
All because one little boy's mom
said it was okay to share.

    [pause]

We praise you, Creator,
and thank you for the fellowship
we enjoy in our congregation
and community.

We praise you, Holy Spirit,
and thank you for the strength
to go work in our community.

We praise you, Lord Jesus,
and thank you for the bread and cup
you share so generously
so everyone gets fed,
for You tell us it's okay to share.

Thank you, God, Thank you.

Amen.

8/9/15
Matthew 14:13-21

God, Demons are Scary

God, demons are scary.
And hard
to get rid of!

They cause us to writhe
and do that which we don't want to do,
scattering our hopes and dreams
with shouts and rages.

We try, Lord, we really do
try to get rid of them
ourselves.
But it doesn't work.

Prayer works. Prayers
to have God remove
that which remains
untouchable.

Let us pray, then,
that the demon of racism
be banished and driven out
by the clearing of our eyes
to see how we participate.

Let us pray, then,
that the demon of parochialism
be cleansed from us
opening our hearts
to overcome divisions.

Let us pray, today,
that the demon of fear
fade into smoke
as we look to our future
with the light of the world
guiding us always!

Thank you, God, Thank you.

Amen.

8/16/15
Luke 9:37-43

Bread of Life

God, in our world,
eating the flesh of a neighbor
would be frowned upon.

Yet we devour every scrap
of news and detail
about celebrities large and small.
We eat up gossip
like a rich dessert!

Who's the cannibal now
I wonder?

But in your world,
the bread of life is real,
sustaining and nourishing us eternally.

Jesus, you call us,
beckoning, offering,
swaying, sustaining,
everlasting, good to the last bite,
sweet nectar, rich meaty flavor,
thirst-quenching taste
love.

Lord, you make us lick
our lips with anticipation
and delight!
Finger-licking good,
you are the real
good news food.

We pray for those all around us
suffering from simple
physical hunger: we'll help
feed them whenever we can.

We pray for the soldiers
fighting out of loyalty and honor;
bring them home safely.

We pray for the hungry souls
searching for meaning
in a confusing world;
be with us all always.

Thank you, God, thank you.

Amen.

8/19/12
John 6:51-58

And We Reply

Jesus, there is a fog covering
the ground this morning,
blanketing us all alike-
friend, neighbor, homeless
and elderly.

Sometimes, Lord, even when
this earthly fog clears we
find our thoughts are foggy still.
It makes it hard
to answer questions, it
makes it hard to know
just what is.

You ask us,
"Who do you say that I am?"

And we reply, mostly without thinking,
You are Christ, Son of the living God...
My dad told me that,
my Sunday School teacher with the
short stockings told me that;
my pastor told me that.

Yes, but
who do *you* say that I am?

It makes me think of watching
those who weed and mow
the yard, those who
clean the kitchen.

It makes me think of those
who work on Habitat houses
and Child Advocacy, and Hospice
and Play Day and Salvation Army
and on and on.

It makes me think of those
in worship, in fellowship,
in community
because of you.

Thank you, God, thank you.

Amen.

8/21/11
Matthew 16:13-20

Lord, She's Here Again

Lord, she's here again.
That woman, hovering,
clawing for a break.
Hungry as a ravenous lion
for any scrap.

And she's not even one of us!

Let her mind her
manners at someone else's table
but she yaps back
like a dog
claiming at least a scrap.

She, lifted up and
we, brought down,
meet in respect and mutuality.

Father, we pray this day
for your guidance and blessing.
Direct us in all we do
to remember you.

Holy Wisdom, we pray this day
for strength and good humor
as we go out into our community
on Faith in Action Sunday.

Eternal Creator, we pray this day
for peace. Peace for the meek
and the strong, for the weak and the brave,
for the lost and the leader.

Thank you, God, thank you!

Amen.

8/24/14
Mark 7:24-30

We Are One in Christ

Lord, we can get
so tangled up in rules
about who can speak
and who can't.
Your servant, Paul,
put it succinctly,
in Christ, you are one -
get over yourself!

And yet, we persist
in trying to find an edge,
something to set us apart,
better, more holy, more righteous.

So much so
we overlook and forget:
we are one in Christ.

We pray with desire
to do your will
in all that we do during
Faith in Action Sunday.
May we be a real blessing
in our community.

We pray with hope
to do your will always;
guide us in our vision and mission.

We pray with patience
to do your will
as we prepare for
Trick r Trunk and the Bazaar.
May your love guide us
in all we do.

Thank you, God, thank you!

Amen.

8/31/14
Romans 16:1-16;
Galatians 3:26-28.
1 Corinthians14:33-35

Fall Season

A Time for Gratitude and Peace

Tommy gets Honest

Spencerville is catching its breath after the Labor Day festivities and parade. It's not really fall yet but it's not summer anymore either. The trees down on Sycamore Rd. still have all their leaves but maybe a few are beginning to turn yellow. The breeze seems to shake them a little harder and after a rain, there's a few more on the ground. Still, it'll be at least another month before they turn fully, and pumpkins occupy the storefronts and porches around the Square and the Buttermilk Café' puts the old scarecrow out to guard the entrance.

That'll come along in due time, but it all takes me back to the time Elvira and Bo were talking over a cup of mild roast as I came into the Café with Tommy. He'd agreed to meet with me to talk over a few things that were bothering me. My grandmother had died a few weeks before and, while I wasn't totally devastated, I wasn't really good either; and I didn't know what to do about it.

Now, it's not like I had never been to a funeral or to church for that matter, but I couldn't seem to find the words that would say what I was feeling. I wasn't even sure I should be feeling what I was feeling. But I knew I needed to talk to somebody about it and Tommy was about the best listener I ever met. The strange thing was he never seemed to tire of listening. Heck, I'd be checking my watch for how much longer I was going to go on and on and he'd still be smiling and listening! But it wasn't like that this day as I wasn't even sure where to start.

"Thanks for coming, Tommy, I appreciate it. Can I get you a cup of coffee?"

"Sure - hey, Elvira, two cups of coffee - you stay seated, I'll get 'em - Bo, could you pass me the creamer?" he answered. Elvira didn't even pause - just waved her hand and kept beating Bo's ear about Mayor Stevens and how he'd stirred things up again at the Council meeting last week.

With coffee sweetened and altered to suit my taste, I tried to get started.

"So. My grandmother Jean died a few weeks ago and I went home for the funeral last week." I said.

"I'm so sorry, Scott," Tommy relied gently.

"Thanks, Tommy. I'm okay with it except... well, except... I think I'm a real jerk."

Tommy didn't say anything but the look on his face and the head tilt said, "How so?"

Where to start when the real truth is you feel relieved when someone dies? My grandmother was old - 91 - she'd lived a long life but not so much around me. I probably only saw her a few times after I got out of college and she moved to the Nursing Home in Kansas City. And even when we did see each other, it was mostly out of politeness and courtesy. Sure, she was family, but she hadn't been around much when I was growing up and we just didn't have much of a relationship. Everyone cried at her funeral, but I wasn't sure why I was crying. You see?

I said, "I wasn't particularly close to her and while it's sad and all, I just feel relieved and then that makes me feel guilty. I mean am I just thinking about myself, one less Birthday to remember? How selfish is that? I'd pray but what can I say? I can't tell God that..."

Tommy smiled and looked through or over my shoulder like someone interesting just came in the room and I almost turned around to look. His eyes focused back on mine and he asked, "How do you pray? How do you talk to God?"

"I don't know, something like, 'Dear God, I pray for my grandmother Jean and for my folks... in Jesus' name, amen?" I said with shrug.

Tommy smiled and said nothing. We each took a sip of our coffee and stared at the plates for a moment. I knew better than to read anything into his pauses - I never knew where he went in those gaps but wherever it was, it gave him strength and hope.

"You're afraid God might see who you really are rather than the image you so hope is who he wants you to be, huh?" Tommy said abruptly. I blinked. Twice.

'Well... maybe." I whispered.

And then Tommy told me his story. He said,

"Yeah, I know what you mean. I think I've told you how my folks died in a car accident when I was 18 and how bitter and cold I was about that. I wanted God to take the blame, I wanted God to feel what I felt. But I couldn't say that to God, to Jesus. You're supposed to be grateful for Jesus loves you - 'Jesus loves me this I know, for the Bible tells me so...' I couldn't put what I felt into the words of that kind of song, that kind of thankful prayer. So I stopped trying. I stopped feeling. I told myself, 'It'll get better, I'm tough.' And I believed that, and I really thought I was okay, and it was getting better.

But it didn't. I'd wake up angry wanting to shout, 'You go to Hell, God, you go to Hell!'

"And then one night, I did say that - right out loud and I started to cry and cry and say everything I was trying to keep from showing, everything I didn't want to deal with. Everything I held onto to protect myself. But somehow that night, I let it go, dropped all the baggage."

Tommy paused a little then and finally said quietly, "It wasn't until then that I felt Jesus' tears drip beside mine, softening the edges of my pain as if to say, "I know... I know."

Tommy told me, "Prayer means being able to say that to God. It means being able to say it to myself. If you can't be honest with yourself - how can you be honest with God?"

The next time I took a sip of coffee, it was cold. Tommy was still there, smiling like he didn't have a care in the world and, for all I know, he didn't. I mean, if you could be honest enough to tell God off, is there anything you couldn't share with God?

Like a Wayward Child

Like a wayward child, God,
we pout and cry and whine
about our perceived injustices,
sure that we have been wronged,
sure that we are right...

while the ones we have wronged
wait for our recognition
and apology; a simple
"I'm sorry" will do,
thank you very much.

And neither approach,
if taken insincerely,
can ever really lead
to the reconciliation
that You desire, God.

With sighs too deep for words,
we sometimes find
this part of our lives too hard
to do and understand.

Can we leave the judging to you, God?

Can we leave off the hatred
and pain? Can we really
conquer evil with good?

Throughout our world
there are wars and civil wars
and insurrections and tribal fights;
we pray for your peace
to rule them all.

Throughout our country
there are political fights

and congressional bottlenecks
and stalemates and logjams;
we pray your patience and hope
in the halls of government.

Throughout our community
there are people struggling
for work, for food, for justice;
we pray your strength
be with us
as we journey
with them.

Thank you, God, thank you.

Amen.

9/4/11
Matthew 18:15-20

Lord, this is Hard for Us

God, we have seen so many people this week,
we have smiled and talked and
smiled some more!

We surely hope we've entertained a few angels!
Certainly, we've beautified
more than a few princesses!

Relationships.
You come to us in relationship,
don't you, God?
So the way we welcome
our visitors and neighbors and friends
is the way we welcome you.

In you, there are no differences,
no 'us' or 'them', no enemies.
Lord, this is hard for us.

Could we free Onesimus
as Paul asked Philemon to do?

As Paul asks us to do?

We pray today, father, for those
in our town who are hungry,
who have no job,
maybe not even a place to live.

We pray, Jesus, that
we can show your love
through our mission and outreach
here, nationally, and across your
whole
world.

We will welcome
the stranger as you have
welcomed us.

Thank you for this chance, God.
Strengthen us. Calm us. Love us.

Thank you, God, thank you.

Amen.

9/5/10
Philemon 1:1-21

Still You Send Us

God, you ask
"Whom shall I send?" and we try to answer
"Here I am, send me!"
But God, I've got to get
the oil changed first
and the dry cleaning
needs dropped off
and, well...
my calendar's really full
this week but next Wednesday
looks okay...

Sometimes, that's our story
and Lord, how we tell it!
Even when we think
we're saying nothing
the truth comes out
in our actions and foibles.

Still you send us-
'Go - tell your stories,
share with all you can,
share with those who
welcome you and those
who don't.'

But we're not sure
we even have a story
let alone how to share it.

Go anyway.

We pray dear Father,
for strength and hope,
for perseverance when the way
seems dark.

We pray holy Mother,
for your love
to guide us and give us wisdom.

We pray deepest Mystery,
silence our selfish thoughts
so our story
may be shared
with clarity and truth
in all that we do.

Thank you, God, thank you!

Amen.

9/8/13
Luke 9:57-10:11

But We Doubt

Mother God, you've held us
and calmed our fears
and wiped our runny noses
and bandaged our hurts
and loved us unconditionally
when we're ignored or pushed down
or made to feel small.

Is this how you love yourself?

Christ Jesus, your self-giving love,
there for all, especially
the poor and weak, the lost and lonely,
is the deepest and richest love
we can ever have.

But we doubt; we look
for a better deal,
a richer friend,
something - anything
to guarantee success!
Like the rich old fool,
we build barns and houses
big enough to hold a future
that may never come.
All the while
turning our backs to the present
and it's needs and joys
right beside us.

Lord, there are those
in our congregation who
have lost loved ones
and we pray for their sorrow.
Bring them hope and gentle peace.

Teacher, there are those
in our community who,
through no fault of their own,
always seem to come up short.
We pray for clear eyes to see
that they are us on some other day;
their needs are no different than ours.

Eternal Father, there are those
in our lives who
we shun and ignore, favoring
a greener field
across another fence.
We pray for forgiveness
for our lack of faith.

Thank you, God, thank you.

Amen.

9/9/12
James 2:1-10,14-17

Be with Us, Lord

God, Creator, Higher Power
of our understanding,
help us to 'let go and let God'
one day at a time.

You have shown us a way of life
that is so much more than
we ever thought possible.
You have brought us
out of bondage and into a life
of happiness, joy and freedom!

We celebrate that freedom today.
We ride to enjoy that freedom
with our friends.
But we ride also to honor
our veterans, those who have
given their strength and courage
to defend our country.

Even if they cannot be with us,
we ride with their spirit
surrounding us, going on ahead
like a banner of protection!

So be with us, Lord,
be with us on this beautiful day,
keep us attentive and sharp
to stay safe on our ride.

Keep us happy, joyous and free
for we know
you will guide us even when
we know nothing about it.

Eternal Mystery, there is no place
you cannot find us.

We pray for those still suffering.
We pray for those suffering from
injuries and trauma.
Bring your healing and hope
to all in need.

Thank you, God, thank you!

Amen.

*Central Nebraska Council
on Alcoholism and Addiction (CNCAA)
Freedom Ride - 9/13/14*

How Many Times?

How many times, Lord,
should I forgive?
That many? Sometimes,
I think never
more appropriate.

But you ask in return
"How much have you
been forgiven, child?"
The past won't change
because you won't forgive it
for ever happening.

Forgiveness doesn't keep score.
As you forgive your debtors,
so shall you be forgiven.

Today, Creator, we pray
for our community,
for the homeless and hungry.
Guide us to a successful CROP Walk.

Today, Eternal Light, we pray
for soldiers all over the world.
Bring them home safely;
guide us into the way of peace.

Today, deepest Mystery, we pray
for our church, for continued direction
to do your mission
in the world. Help us
to be the church, to spread the gospel,
to use words if we have to!

Thank you, God, thank you!

Amen.

9/14/14
Matthew 18:21-35

Be Still

Lord, we don't know when
to keep our mouths shut.
The psalmist said,
"Be still, and know that I am God"
while an old wag at an AA meeting said,
"I can tell you're lying
because your lips are moving!"

And there's "Loose lips sink ships."
and "Don't be like
the boy who cried wolf."
or "If you can't say something good;
say nothing at all."

A key component of communication
is that someone be listening.
Are we choosing to not listen
to you, Mysterious Light,
by the volume of our speech?

Remind us once again
to be still. And silent sometimes.

      [*pause*]

We pray for the peace
to know your presence, Lord.
We long to know your touch,
your healing touch.
Bring healing and hope to all
of our recovering people;
bring patience to those facing surgery too.

Master, we pray also
for everyone who serves through
Habitat for Humanity.
Together, we help make
a better world.

God, we pray for our
soldiers and our representatives
far away from home.
The least spark can fire passions
that explode, whether naturally
or with evil help. We pray for
reason rather than reaction,
peace rather than partisanship,
hope rather than bleak terror.

Thank you, God, thank you.

Amen.

9/16/12
James 3:1-12

Welcome the Visitors

Our forefather, Abraham,
dozing in the midday sun, caught
sleeping, keeping, watching
not so well,

Still, he
knew how to greet
a stranger.

Asking forgiveness and
offering huge, abundant generosity,
he wiped the sleep from his eyes,

And welcomed the visitors.

We pray, O God, that we
can wipe the sleepy safeness
of family from our eyes
to see - and greet - the stranger
among us.

We pray, O God, that we
can labor without the burden
of judgement,
that we can forgive
without keeping score.

Jesus, the great forgiver,
greeted all - invited all -
going from shore to shore
to share bread in
huge, abundant generosity.

We pray, O God, that we
can savor the gifts
of your grace
with happiness and joy!

For it is in community
and sharing
that we know your love.

Thank you, God, thank you.

Amen.

9/21/08
Matthew 20:1-16

Love One Another

Love. You tell us to love.
Love you,
love our neighbors as ourselves,
love one another.

Love, it's always and only
love!

Yet this hellish world
we live in
surrounds us-
we're not kind,
we're envious and we love to boast.
We can be rude and arrogant,
insisting on our own way.
We get irritated and resentful
and take pleasure in doing wrong.
The truth is a stranger to us.

We're not very good
at relationships, God.

So we pray for forgiveness.
With humble hearts,
we repent and turn back to you.
May we bless visitors
as you have blessed us.

We pray for strength.
With willing hearts,
we repent and turn back to you.
May our hard work bless our community
as you have blessed us.

We pray with thanksgiving.
Our thankful hearts
reach out across our congregation
as we gather each Sunday
to share your peace
in our fellowship.

Thank you, God, Thank you.

Amen.

9/27/15
1 Corinthians 13:1-8a

Choices

God, we heard about your party.
But we've got something else
on the calendar for that day...
Can we take a rain check?

    [pause]

Lord, it's getting cooler now
and the shelter's full,
I'll have lunch
at Salvation Army
to warm me up
and yes, I'd be delighted
to come to your party!

    [pause]

Choices present themselves
sometimes making us think-
but usually we react
in the surety that we know best.

In those times, your patience
is tested, isn't it Creator?

We've much to pray for though
so we pray for your guidance
and help as we face
choices and decisions
about a leaky roof.
Lord, the rain is welcome,
just not in the fellowship hall!

We pray this day for peace-
a peace we will
try to leave in your trust.

We pray this season
with thankfulness for your
abundance,
a generosity
that makes it easy to give.
Yours is a generosity that
doesn't give up
in the face of busy schedules and
personal desires.

Thank you, God, thank you.

Amen.

10/09/11
Matthew 22:1-14

I Wanted To

God, I planned on taking some time
this morning to sit in quiet prayer
but...

I really wanted to try to listen,
I wanted to be still and know
that you are
God
but...

I had plans I'd made
and they had to be fulfilled.

Like the wedding guests,
when it came time,
I had other plans.

I wanted to feed the hungry
but I had other plans,

I wanted to visit the sick
but I had other plans,

I wanted to,

I wanted,

I...

But like the strangers
surprising Abram at the Oaks of Mamre,
you come anyway.

There will be a banquet!

Creator, help us to un-plan
our lives so there's room
for the hungry, for the sick,
and for the just plain lonely.

Father, help us be ready to
feed our mothers, old now.

Mother, show us the ways
to help our fathers who cannot
take care of themselves
any longer.

God, help us to leave
more of our lives
in your hands
and less to our plans.

Thank you, God, thank you.

Amen.

10/12/08
Matthew 22:1-14

Take Our Stoney Hearts

Creator, giver of life
and soul, deepening our hearts
daily inspiring love,
we gather together
to praise you and glorify your name.

Then we gossip about each other
as though you weren't here!

Wash us clean, God.
Take our stoney hearts
and recreate them
with purity and humility.

The air is crisper today, Lord,
and the leaves are beginning
to turn into a palette of color.
Snow will come, blanketing
the world white; make our hearts
as clean as fresh snow.

We pray this morning
for guidance on all levels.
We pray for our leaders;
we pray for hope.

We pray this morning
for children,
for their safety and happiness.

We pray this morning
for peace - in our homes, in our jobs,
in our nation and in
your world.

Thank you, God, thank you.

Amen.

10/13/13
Psalm 51:1-15

A Both-And Kind of Guy

God, the world and all of its stuff
swirl around us
all the time!
Makes it hard to keep
our heads on straight.

Makes it hard to know the difference
between either-or
and
both-and.

Jesus, you're a
both-and kind of guy, aren't you?
Confounding Pharisees
and us alike
in our Empire clothes
and Empire political scheming
you point to the prize
you prize most.

"Give to God
that which is God's"
you tell us.

So we bow in prayer, recalling
the psalmist who admonished us,
"A king is not saved by his great army;
a warrior is not delivered by his great strength."*

We bow in prayer for blessing
on this year's CROP Walk–
may we walk all over
poverty.

We bow in prayer of thanks
for the fellowship
and goodwill shared

through our Bazaar-
may the monies raised
be a blessing in its use.

We bow our heads in prayers
of thankfulness that you
invite us into your kingdom,
your vineyard, your
wedding banquet.

Thank you, God, thank you.

Amen.

10/16/11
Matthew 22:15-22

*Psalm 33:16

Help Us to Keep Focused

Dear God, my mind is so cluttered
right now
I can't think of anything to say.
No wonder the prophets
and Jesus went off
alone to pray.

Dark nights under the stars
at Gethsemane,
Jesus prayed
and the disciples
couldn't stay awake.

We feel so good
when we give to you, O God
but we seem to keep
more to ourselves.

Our lives are cluttered
like a Galilean marketplace,
like the money changers in the Temple,
like my desk.

Too much to do,
too much stuff.
It is no surprise that
we have trouble feeling
centered
in you.

Help us, God, to keep
our eyes focused
on our mission.

We'll help others so they will
know your help through us.

We'll feed others so they will
know your nourishment through us.

We'll comfort others so they will
know your love through us.

Give us the discipline to
stay focused on you
rather than our clutter
no matter how it sparkles
and beckons.

For in you, O God of mystery,
we find our best strength
and our deepest love.

Thank you, God, thank you.

Amen.

10/19/08
Matthew 22:15-22

Abundance

In the still darkness
of morning,
starlight shines gently
across corn stubble and fields
now empty; harvested.

God, the rains were good this year,
your sun paced the summer
and filled our crops
with your energy.

Creator, we know your
abundance overflows
but we stumble in these
hard economic times;
for many, making ends meet
feels like abundance!

Then we realize that your abundance
often comes in the chances
we have to do something
for someone else.

This week, Lord, we've seen
that abundance
in our offerings of service
to Salvation Army,
and Habitat for Humanity,
The sharing of blessings
at the Church Foundation workshop
and the fun
of an Eagle Scout project!

We've seen it in donations to
our little pantry
and in the relief
in the eyes of those who need it.

You have truly blessed us,
from generation to generation!

Thank you, God, thank you.

Amen.

10/23/11
Deuteronomy 34:1-12

Like the Rich Young Man

God, remember the hymn we all
learned as children?
"Jesus loves me, this I know,
for the Bible tells me so..."

Do you really love us?

With all your heart?
and with all your soul,
and with all your mind?

Do you really love us like that?

The psalmist says, "Be still and know"
but my life is so cluttered
I feel such a need
to be in control.

Like the rich young man
who leaves Jesus because
he's just not sure he can
let go of his possessions,
we hold onto
our needs and wants,
we grip the reigns of control
and power
thinking this will
fulfill us, satisfy us.

But it doesn't.

Not nearly so much as
finding you, O God,
looking back at us from the eyes
of a little child who needs a hug.
Or from the smile of an
old woman in a nursing home.

O God, we pray for all
your children who will
go unloved today.

Help us to be the face of love,
the heart and soul and mind
of your love in the world today.

I read it in the Bible,
you love us, don't you?

Thank you, God, thank you.

Amen.

10/26/08
Matthew 22:34-46

You Are There

Eternal Creator,
Like a solid rock
unshakable even by the moon,
You are there.

Like a comet returning
over and over and over through centuries,
You are there.

Sometimes, we may
even look up and notice.

Like a pop bottle
recovered from the ditch
by the side of our road,
You redeem us and clean us new.

God, what a great day
of hospitality!
Trick 'r Trunk was our 'oaks of Mamre'
and we thank you for the chance
to provide extravagant hospitality to our neighbors.

God, what a great day
this day as we celebrate
life and the joy it brings.

God, what a great day
to pray for healing and hope
for our brothers and sisters
in hospital or home
facing illness and recovery.

Thank you, God, thank you!

Amen.

10/27/13
Psalm 19

Under the Oaks at Mamre

Lord, some strangers
came by last night.
Dressed as minions,
they took our candy and ran!

But we welcomed them anyway,
just like a dusty, dry
day under the oaks at Mamre.

Were you there?
Are you there?
Whenever we think
we're safe and sound
and comfortable with
food and shelter to spare?

      [*pause*]

We pray this day, Creator,
for our church, for guidance
and strength as we continue
to be your church.

We pray this day, Holy Wisdom,
for your comfort and peace,
knowing that our faith and trust
is enough,
even when we have
no clue.

We pray this day, Abba,
for our world.
Tossed and lost in turmoil,
fear can overwhelm us -
and then the stranger scares us.
Lead us by right paths
and still waters.

Thank you, God, Thank you.

Amen.

11/01/15
Genesis 18:1-8

The Voice

Loving God, to you
we give our praise.
You have trusted us
with life and with stewardship.
We are your sheep
and we know your voice.

It's different, it's not
the voice of gold or silver
fashioned into idols
to be spent on trinkets.

It's gentle, it's not
the strident voice of judgement
or anger.

It's peaceful, it's not
a cry of attack
or of retreat.

It's the voice of our
Rock and Redeemer.

We pray this morning, Lord,
for all who serve you
through Habitat or Salvation Army.
We are your stewards
of home and hearth.

We pray this morning, Father,
for those serving our nation
all around the world.
We pray for peace
so all soldiers may return
to their families.

We pray this morning, Creator,
with thanks
for your generosity and patience.

Thank you, God, thank you!

Amen.

11/03/13
Psalm 115:1-8

Love Comes First

Jesus, the other day
a driver cut me off
as I was turning into the Mall.
It's not fair!
But as I steamed about it,
I heard someone beep as
I drove right in front of them!
It wasn't fair, Lord.
No, it wasn't.

You're not too big
on fairness; love
comes first with you.

Thank you, God,
for loving me all those times
when it would have been
fair to not love me.

Blessed are the meek and abandoned
for they are beloved by God.
Blessed are the persecuted and wronged;
God loves them.
Blessed are the tax collectors
and politicians;
God loves them too.

Creator, you rain down your love on the just and unjust,
the weak and the strong.
National and tribal boundaries
cannot bind or direct you!

This day, Eternal Light,
we pray for peace
for all of us - our kind
and our enemies.

This day, loving Father,
we pray for those
recovering from Hurricane Sandy.
We will assemble Hygiene kits
with prayers of hope.

This day, sweet Wisdom,
we pray for those suffering
illness and loss. Their sorrow
pains us too and we cry out
with them for strength and relief
and healing.

Thank you, God, thank you.

Amen.

11/04/12
Matthew 5:38-48

Thanksgiving Every Day

God, Thanksgiving is coming soon.
The holiday, I mean!
We'll be traveling or preparing
for family and turkey,
dressing and cranberry sauce,
peas with little onions
and pumpkin pie, of course.

I wonder, do we
do ourselves an injustice
by focusing our thanks
on one day?

Do we save up our
thanksgivings for
that day while the psalmist
says, 'come into God's presence
with thanksgiving'?

Thinking back,
we look forward to
our stewardship
with gratitude;
we are the people
of Your pasture
and the sheep of Your hand.

It is with thanksgiving
that we pray for all
who serve at Salvation Army.
Their joy can brighten
someone else's life.

It is with thanksgiving
that we pray for all
struck down by the sudden typhoon
in the Philippines.

Especially in shock and sorrow,
we are strengthened by your
grace and love.

And it is with thanksgiving
that we rejoice,
making a joyful noise
for the satisfaction
of serving as your stewards,
loving Creator.

Thank you, God, thank you!

Amen.

11/10/13
Psalm 95

They Were Lovers of Peace

God, we honor our veterans today and tomorrow.
Not so much because they
were warriors
but rather because they were lovers
of peace and hope.
They fought out of duty and loyalty.
They fought afraid and scared
and many came home scarred.

But thy will be done
in all things
whether we know it or not.

Abba, you are there
when no one else is,
in the darkness of night,
in the bright shining day.

We glorify your name
and rejoice in your will
which guides us better
than we can ourselves.

Forgive us, Mother, for we have sinned.
Forgive us just as much
as we're willing to forgive.

We leave our offerings aside
to make up with those
we've belittled or angered
for repaired relationship
means more to you than
hollow worship.

You provide us with
an abundant table, overflowing
like a cup too full!

Today, some veteran,
somewhere will be cold and hungry.
Maybe they've hidden themselves
or are lost in horrors
they can't seem to shake.
We pray especially for them today, God.
Please stamp their tests
as complete and passed.

Thank you, God, thank you.

Amen.

11/11/12 - Veterans Day
Matthew 6:1-24

Letting Go

Moses asked, "Why Me?
I don't have any special talents."

And you said, "I trust you."

Likewise, Jesus never
told anyone they weren't
qualified, he simply said,
"Come, and follow me."

And many did,
the sick and lonely,
the tax collector and the
adulterous woman,

And Mary and Martha,
and Zaccheus.

But - some didn't.

Why is it God, that
we have such trouble
letting go?

Why do our fears keep us
shackled, unable to take
risks and go out on a limb
for you?

Why do we bury our talents
keeping them hidden
when they could
help a neighbor,
feed a hungry child,
let someone know they're
not forgotten?

Why do we accuse you
of being mean when we're
the ones holding back?

Please have patience with us, God.

We pray for your care
and strength, we pray
with thanks for your love.

Amen.

11/16/08
Matthew 25:14-30

Bless Our Hearts, Lord

Bless our hearts, Lord,
bless us all!

God, we stand in your sight
as judge and jury.
We know each smudge
and speck
in our neighbor's eye
yet fail so much as to glance
at the mirror in passing.

And worries? Lord, lord
we've got them.
Will that sorry excuse
for a cousin behave
after Thanksgiving dinner this year?
Bless their heart.

And what clothes shall
we wear, what balance
between show and comfort
for a long day of
turkey and television?

In the meantime, Everlasting Master,
we pray you be with us today
as we prepare hygiene kits
for Church World Service
to help with cleanup after
Hurricane Sandy.

Eternal Mystery,
we pray you be with us today
as we smile and greet
friends and visitors. Help us
to realize our hospitality is a
reflection of yours.

Abba and Amma, we pray
be with us as we
rejoice with thanksgiving
in the coming week,
thankful ever for your
grace and mercy.

Thank you, God, thank you.

Amen.

11/18/12
Matthew 6:25-7:14

We Thank You, Lord

God - the fruits of Thanksgiving are over
for good or bad;
families have gathered
or not, blessing food and hearts
with equal passion!

We thank you, Lord,
for your grace and mercy.
Most of the time.
If we have to.

Yet you come to us
again and again,
never turning aside.
You are like the rock
at the base of a sturdy house,
weathering the storms of life
with ease.

We thank you and pray
for the Crisis Center
and Hope Harbor
and Salvation Army
who help the homeless and weak.

We thank you and pray
for the little children
dazzled by toys and decorations.
they are too young
to know the difference between
good fruit and bad fruit.
Help us to teach them.

We thank you and pray
for peace. Peace
on the battlefield.
peace in our hearts.
The peace of Christ
offered anew each day.

Thank you, God, thank you.

Amen.

11/25/12
Matthew 7:15-29

Scripture Index

Genesis
6:9-22, 7:24, 8:14-19   Forgive Our Foolishness, 101
16:1-4, 18:9-15, 21:1-19   As You Promised, 123
18:1-8   Abundant Hospitality, 42
    Under the Oaks at Mamre, 190
22:1-14   But You're Not, 114
28:10-17   Jacob's Stone Pillow, 34

Deuteronomy
34:1-12   Abundance, 185

Joshua
2:1-21, 6:22-25   Blind Like Jesus, 127

Ruth
1:1-17a   Kernels of Hope, 141

2 Samuel
11:1-5   Help Us to See, 135

Psalms
19   You Are There, 189
51:1-15   Take Our Stoney Hearts, 180
85:1-2, 8-13   In Preparation, 21
95   Thanksgiving Every Day, 196
115:1-8   The Voice, 192

Isaiah
40:1-11   In Preparation, 21
60:1-6   An Epiphany of Light, 36

Jeremiah
31:31-34   We Confess, 64

Jonah
1:1-3a, 17-2:6   What if Everyone Repents?, 116

Matthew

2:1-12	An Epiphany of Light, 36
2:12-23	On the Run Again, 30
3:13-17	A Voice was Heard in Ramah, 38
	You Know What's Funny, God?, 44
4:1-11	Obedience is as Obedience Does, 58
5:13-16	Salt and Light, 111
5:21-26	O Lord, Hear Our Prayers, 119
5:27-32	Pray for Us Sinners, 125
5:38-48	Love Comes First, 194
6:1-24	They Were Lovers of Peace, 198
6:25-7:14	Bless Our Hearts, Lord, 202
7:15-29	We Thank You, Lord, 204
14:13-21	And the World was Fed, 143
14:22-33	The Water is a Scary Place, 139
16:13-20	And We Reply, 148
17:1-9	Transfigured, 51
18:15-20	Like a Wayward Child, 159
18:21-35	How Many times?, 169
20:1-16	Welcome the Visitors, 172
21:28-32	You Do Not Fit Well into Boxes, 109
22:1-14	Choices, 176
	I Wanted To, 178
22:15-22	A Both-And Kind of Guy, 181
	Help Us to Keep Focused, 183
22:34-46	Like the Rich Young Man, 187
25:14-30	Letting Go, 200
28:1-10	Suddenly, 78
28:16-20	Re-collected, 88

Mark

1:4-11	I Am Forgiven, 40
1:21-28	We Pray Your Realm Comes Soon, 50
7:24-30	Lord, She's Here Again, 150

Luke
1:67-79	Our Loving God, 24
2:1-20	The Gift, 28
2:8-20	They Went to See, 32
2:41-51	You Do Not Fit Well into Boxes, 109
3:1-6	Preparing the Way, 23
9:37-43	God, Demons are Scary, 144
9:57-10:11	Still You Send Us, 163
10:25-37	Go and Do Likewise, 129
	Who is Our Neighbor?, 133
12:13-21	Think About Today, 137
24:13-35	I Wouldn't Recognize You, 74

John
2:1-11	And the Wine Flows, 46
2:13-22	Turning About, 60
4:5-42	Anything Can Happen at a Well, 62
5:1-9	Change is Hard, Lord, 92
6:51-58	Bread of Life, 146
9:1-41	How Many Times Must I Tell You?, 68
	Your Light Will Show, 72
10:1-10	In the Worrying, 76
12:12-16	Deliverance from Blindness, 66
12:20-33	We Confess, 64
14:15-24	Stewardship is a Gift, 80
	In Memoriam, 95
17:6-19	for Our Sins are Great, 86
20:1-18	Peace Be With You, 70
20:19-23	The Sound of the Wind, 105

Acts
2:1-21	Just One Spirit, 94
3:1-10, 4:1-21	For the Times He Was Bold, 107
9:1-25	A Call of Creation, 113
11:1-18	Your Spirit at Work, 82
	A Surprising God, 84
16:16-34	Mother to Us All, 90

Romans
16-1-16   We Are One in Christ, 151

1 Corinthians
8:1-13   Guide Us, Lord, 48
13:1-8a   Love One Another, 174
14:33-35   We Are One in Christ, 151

Galatians
1:11-24   We Praise You, God, 103
3:25-28, 5:1   Set Us Free, 118
                                We Are One in Christ, 151

Colossians
1:1-14   Another Day, 121
2:6-15   Thin Space, 131

Philemon
1:1-21   Lord, This is Hard for Us, 161

James
2:1-10, 14-17   But We Doubt, 165
3:1-12   Be Still, 170

1 John
5:9-13   for Our Sins are Great, 86

www.ingramcontent.com/pod-product-compliance
Lightning Source LLC
Chambersburg PA
CBHW072006110526
44592CB00012B/1225